The Reading Workshop
Creating Space for Readers

FRANK SERAFINI

Heinemann
Portsmouth, NH

Heinemann
A division of Reed Elsevier Inc.
361 Hanover Street
Portsmouth, NH 03801-3912
www.heinemann.com

Offices and agents throughout the world

Library of Congress Cataloging-in-Publication Data

Serafini, Frank.
  The reading workshop : creating space for readers / Frank Serafini.
    p. cm.
  Includes bibliographical references and index.
  ISBN 0-325-00330-0 (pbk.)
  1. Reading (Elementary). I. Title.

LB1573 .S453 2001
372.4—dc21   2001016965

Editor: Lois Bridges
Production: Elizabeth Valway
Cover design: Jenny Jensen Greenleaf, Greenleaf Illustration & Design
Manufacturing: Steve Bernier

Printed in the United States of America on acid-free paper
11 10 09 08   VP   10 11 12

This book is dedicated to Dr. Seuss
for providing a door
into the world of literature,
and to my parents
for giving me the key.

Contents

Foreword

There are many paths to teaching reading—how does a teacher begin to make sense of all the different approaches that are available?

Teachers should begin with Frank Serafini's *The Reading Workshop: Creating Space for Readers*. Frank's book will give you the opportunity to take a mental tour of his wonderful classroom and reader's workshop. On this tour, you can eavesdrop on conversations the children are having about their favorite books and poems, you can see how Frank's classroom is arranged to support a community of readers and writers, and you'll feel the deep sense of connection his students have with books and each other. Then, with this clear portrait in mind of what a reader's community looks and feels like, you can read Frank Serafini's practical strategies for how to create such a community in any classroom.

Frank Serafini's love of teaching and reading illuminate this inspiring and practical book on the reader's workshop. Each insight is informed by his work with his own students, as well as his love of literature and extensive knowledge of the art of teaching reading.

I was particularly struck by how every practical suggestion Frank offers is true to his philosophy of not only helping students become better readers, but also guiding them in making lifelong connections between their lives and the literature they are reading.

Every teacher will take to heart Frank's gentle guidance on how to create an environment where children and books intersect in the most natural of ways, and I'm positive that *The Reading Workshop: Creating Space for Readers* will give teachers the inspiration and guidance they might be searching for to create their own reader's community.

Georgia Heard

Acknowledgments

The path I have traveled in my life is filled with extraordinary people, without whom I would not be the person I am today. Most important, I would like to thank my parents, who allowed me to do what I needed to do in my life, even when it made them nervous. Thank you for all of your support.

To my sister, Suzette, teacher, friend, and sibling rival, may we always be as close as we have been. My Little Haiku.

In my educational journey, I have met some teachers that constantly astound me with their caring and commitment to the lives of children.

To Carolyn Rogers, who helped me get started many years ago, I couldn't have asked for a better mentor and friend.

To Bob Dooley, principal of Discovery School, who has unconditionally supported the style of teaching this book promotes, even when it is politically challenging, thanks for letting my philosophy "dance."

To all of the teachers at Discovery School, who have put children first for many years, I am proud to be your colleague.

To my good friend and traveling companion Robert Lievens, who has had to listen to my ideas over long journeys. You, my friend, are the best.

To Patricia Smith, Rebecca Willey, Jennifer Funke, and Joan Stewart, conference partners and good friends, thanks for letting me pick out all the good restaurants. Your conversations and advice have made me a better educator and person.

To Steve Bialostok and Rich Coles, you prove that intelligence and a sense of humor are not mutually exclusive. It is always a pleasure spending time in your company.

To Lyn Searfoss, good friend, educator, and my mentor at Arizona State University. You are the reason I started this journey, and I thank you.

To my niece Chandler Simone, may you grow up with teachers who understand the power of literature and the need to unleash the imagination.

To my editor Lois Bridges, whose gentle advice and encouragement brought out the best in my writing, I appreciate your dedication to this project.

And finally, to Sharon, my love, who understands who I really am; you always keep my feet on the ground and make my life worth living.

Introduction

. . . *cradle me in your hard covers*
and soft words,
rock me gently in your story, and
reveal to me the ripples
in your heart.

FRANK SERAFINI

"'That Sam I am, that Sam I am, I do not like that Sam I am!' That Sam guy really cracks me up." Sophia shares her opinions as she reads from Dr. Seuss' book *Green Eggs and Ham*, walking past a small group of boys crowded around a table. The boys are sitting at a round table, leaning closely together and reading some stories from Jon Sciezka's book *The Stinky Cheese Man and Other Fairly Stupid Tales*. They seem to be enjoying themselves, laughing out loud at the character of the Little Red Hen that has just been eaten by the Giant near the end of Sciezka's book.

Five other children are sitting at a table near the window, wearing headphones, listening to a cassette tape of *Flip Flop Girl*, a novel by Katherine Paterson. Patiently turning the pages, they follow along with the trials and tribulations of yet another one of their favorite independent and troubled heroines in one of Paterson's new novels.

Another group of children are gathered together on the floor discussing their ideas about *James and the Giant Peach*, by Roald Dahl. These children have chosen to read this book together and are discussing how much they dislike the two aunts in the story, Sponge and Spiker.

Still another group of children are finishing an adaptation of *Wilfred Gordon McDonald Partridge* by Mem Fox for their version of an episode of the television show *Reading Rainbow*. This episode, designed and directed by the children themselves, will eventually be recorded on videotape and aired later on our classroom television during a presentation for our class and invited guests.

Three children are browsing through the classroom library, which is filled with literally hundreds of titles ranging from *Animalia* to *Zen and the Art of Motorcycle Maintenance*, looking for that "perfect" book to settle down with for their reading time. Besides the extensive central library collection, picture books are prominently displayed in decorated boxes around the room for maximum accessibility. The books in these boxes are organized by theme, genre, author, or illustrator. Some children are looking through a box labeled "Geology" for some resources to support their inquiry project on earthquakes.

I am sitting at a round table with a group of six children creating a character sketch of Winnie Foster, the main character in Natalie Babbitt's novel *Tuck Everlasting*. The sketch showed how Winnie has evolved from an innocent girl, living in the "touch-me-not" cottage, into a brave, savvy imposter, lying in the county jail so that Mae Tuck can make her escape. A heated discussion eventually ensued around the issue of whether Winnie should drink the magical water and live forever, or not.

Around the perimeter of the room, under desks, on couches, and seated on plastic chairs pulled up to round wooden tables, children are reading, discussing, and enjoying the books, magazines, and poetry they have chosen. The soft hum of children's voices and the gentle sounds of jazz music coming from a portable stereo can be heard around the room.

This could be the scene at one of the stylish, modern bookstores springing up in most metropolitan centers in North America, serving cappuccino and playing soft music as people wander around perusing the latest *New York Times* bestseller or searching for a particular title at the information desk. These bookstores have become a contemporary gathering place for people to find their favorite books, discover new titles, and talk with other people about literature and life. However, the scene described above takes place every day in classrooms across the continent, supported by teachers who believe in a literature-based, child-centered approach to reading instruction, sometimes referred to as a "reading workshop."

What to some may look and sound like a chaotic rumble of children's voices and movement is really a well-orchestrated, flexibly scheduled literate community. The creation of the underlying structures and procedures that support this reading workshop takes time, patience, a love of literature, and faith in children as curious, literate human beings trying to understand the world and their place in it. It is a dynamic environment, changing and evolving every day to meet the demands and needs of the approximately twenty-five children and one adult who live within these classroom walls for the duration of the school year.

Students and teachers who are involved in a reading workshop interact differently from their counterparts in a traditional, "sit-in-rows-and-fill-in-the-worksheet"-style classroom. In the reading workshop, teachers and students talk about what is important to them, what they are feeling, and the connections they make between their lives and the literature they read, rather than responding to the "literature activities" created in publishers' teacher manuals. Each day brings new challenges, new celebrations, and a sense of adventure that comes from responding to children rather than to directives found in these manuals.

The creation of the reading workshop is a journey that evolves over time. It does not simply come together during the first week of school, only to be forgotten about as students move on to new activities. Instead, the reading workshop is a flexible structure that continually changes in order to meet the demands of the students and teachers who live within its parameters. As teachers respond to the needs and interests of the children in their classrooms, they are able to create a "space" for children to become capable, lifelong readers. It is this space that is important for readers, enabling them to find their way into the pleasures of reading.

The physical environment and the structures that are introduced during the reading workshop are not entirely responsible for children's development into skillful, lifelong readers. Rather, the success of the reading workshop centers on the love of reading and literature, and the way that this love is shared in this literate community. What drives the reading workshop is the community of readers that is created, or as Frank Smith calls it, "The Literacy Club" (1988).

Literature touches the soul. It illuminates life and lifts the spirit. Literature teaches us not only how to read, but also why we should read. It reaches into our being and helps us to understand our place in the world. The authors who create these stories draw us in as readers and entice us to continue reading for the rest of our lives.

I began this introduction with an excerpt from a poem that I wrote several years ago in an attempt to convey my love of reading and the profound effect literature has had on my life. I carry books in my backpack everywhere I go. Whether down the street each day to work, or while I am off traveling on vacation, I always have a book with me so that I am ready to read whenever the opportunity presents itself. Books fill my shelves and pour over onto the floor of my office. They are piled on the nightstand next to my bed and the counter in my bathroom. More than anything else, the love of reading and the enjoyment of sharing literature is what I hope my students remember after spending time together in our learning community.

As I write this introduction, I am aware of the challenges of writing a book of this nature. I want to help you as classroom teachers develop a flexible framework for your reading workshop that does not limit your creativity, yet still provides a framework for you to work within and be successful. I want to explain how various practices such as literature study groups, read alouds, shared reading, strategy groups, and responding to literature might fit together, and how you can incorporate these elements of reading instruction in your own classroom. I want to provide specific examples of the procedures and strategies that I use, while at the same time being careful not to impose any particular teaching strategies upon you as teachers. Finally, I want to provide ideas that build upon what you already know about teaching and the reading process, while at the same time introducing you to some new approaches that will help you grow as literacy educators.

This book is designed to be a short, easy-to-read handbook that provides a framework for launching and maintaining the reading workshop, as well as a valuable resource for teachers to turn to for more information about the topics presented. The reader needs to understand not only the day-to-day schedule, but also the components that develop over time that make up the reading workshop. These components provide the space and the structure for the workshop that allows children to become confident, successful readers during the course of the school year.

Teaching is not simply the ability to create a fantastic lesson plan for one day; rather, it is the ability to weave various experiences together to form a tapestry that provides the opportunities for children to immerse themselves in quality literature and develop as sophisticated readers.

As A. A. Milne said at the beginning of his book *Winnie the Pooh,* "So perhaps the best thing to do is to stop writing Introductions and get on with the book." So I shall.

1
Inside the Reading Workshop: A Typical Day

*. . . schools shouldn't be about handing down a collection of static
truths to the next generation but about responding to the needs and
interests of the students themselves.*

ALFIE KOHN

It's fifteen minutes after the morning school bell has rung. Students are sitting in pairs on the floor and at tables, sharing the entries they wrote in their literature response logs, which they completed the previous night. As the song "Me and Julio Down by the Schoolyard" by Paul Simon begins to play on the classroom stereo, students realize it is time to finish up sharing their reactions to their readings, put their logs in their cubbies, and gather on the carpet in the front of the room. By the time the song is finishing up, the students are sitting on the floor around my rocking chair, ready to begin our "opening ceremonies."

As usual, I start by saying, "Good morning," and ask them, "Well, what's been happening in your lives?" This allows students to share special events with the entire class. Students relate stories about recent camping trips, newly arrived baby cousins, an outing to Peter Piper Pizza, the score of the weekend softball game, and any other important news from home. We listen carefully to each other, knowing how important it is to get to know one another and to respect the stories and experiences we bring to our learning community.

After we have finished sharing the stories and events in our lives, I reach for my guitar and begin plucking a few notes to see if it is in tune. The student "music director" takes the typed lyrics from the song box and passes them out to each student. This week's song is "House at Pooh Corner," written by Kenny Loggins. This song is a ballad about Winnie the Pooh and his friends in the Hundred Acre

1

Wood. Students sing along with me as I accompany them with the guitar. On Mondays, students listen as I sing the song to them. Tuesdays, we look at the lyrics and talk about what the song means to us and what we think the composer was trying to relate to their audience. By Friday, the students will be singing along with me and playing tambourines, maracas, and other percussion instruments.

After we sing our song, I share the headlines from the local newspaper. We try to keep track of any current events that pertain to us or that we have been interested in. Attendance is taken, announcements are made, and we are ready to begin the reading workshop. I always begin the reading workshop with a read aloud I have chosen specifically to go along with a study we are involved with. On this particular day, I have chosen *The Night of the Gargoyles*, written by Eve Bunting and illustrated by David Weisner. This book is part of a "focus unit," where we have been studying the various types of illustrations found in picture books and their relationship to the written text. The illustrations in this particular book are created with black-and-white charcoal or pencil sketches. From high atop the ledges of buildings in New York City, the gargoyles in this book come to life to gather at the fountains and roam the night. The dark and foreboding pictures add to the ominous mood of this story.

As I finish reading the book, students immediately begin to share their ideas about the story and the illustrations in particular. I turn to a large chart behind my rocking chair and begin to write down some of the ideas that are being discussed.

"The black-and-white drawings make the story more spooky," says one student.

"It reminds me of an old black-and-white monster movie I saw once."

"I think he [David Weisner] lives in New York City because we don't have gargoyles like that here in Phoenix."

"The gargoyles are ugly, but I like them."

These are just some of the ideas my students offer.

As the children continue discussing the book, I make some quick mental notes. The books *Jumanji* and *The Mysteries of Harris Burdick*, by Chris Van Allsburg, would also offer new perspectives in our discussions. *Where the Buffaloes Begin*, written by Olaf Baker and illustrated by Stephen Gammell, and *Rome Antics*, by David Macaulay, would be good books to include in this part of our focus unit as well. Soon we will be discussing other types of media used in picture books, such as colorful paints, but for the time being, we are focusing on these black-and-white illustrations and their relationship to the written text. These ideas about the illustrations will continue to be part of our discussions all year, because of the amount of picture books we read and the importance of the relationships between text and illustrations.

As our discussion winds down, I check my workshop schedule to see who I am meeting with today. Every day, I schedule a short reading conference with five different students before I begin meeting with any strategy or literature study groups. I call over five individual students to my table area and ask them what they have been doing during the reading workshop for the past week. This helps me keep track of what each student is doing, what goals they have set for themselves, and what progress they have been making. It also provides me with the opportunity to see if any problems have arisen. On this day, after I have met with the five students (which takes about fifteen minutes), I am scheduled to meet with the *Whipping Boy* literature study group. They have just finished reading the book and today is the first day for their discussion. This should be exciting.

I say, "Okay, let's get started!" and the class disperses. A group of six children heads over to the listening center, where they are enjoying a collection of poems read aloud by various teachers in our school. I asked several teachers to record their favorite poems on audiotape. The students have been enjoying the teachers' poetry selections and the sound of their voices reading these poems.

Another group heads over to the art supply center. They have just completed a literature study on the book *Abel's Island*, by William Steig, and are creating an illustrated map of what they think the island Abel was stranded on might look like. They will be sharing their artistic creation with the class in a few days. We are all looking forward to their presentation.

Still another nine or so children are headed for various spots in the room, books in hand, for independent or paired reading. They have chosen their partners and their own books. They assume the responsibility to make good choices about what they are reading and make sure they have selected enough reading materials to remain engaged for the entire block of time.

I sit in with the literature study group reading *Whipping Boy*, written by Sid Fleischmann, for about twenty minutes. The discussion begins with students sharing their favorite parts of the story and soon turns to issues of fairness, as students express their concerns about Jemmy, the whipping boy, having to endure another whipping for the actions of Prince Brat. It doesn't take long for students to share examples of perceived injustices in their lives or in their experiences at school. We decide as a group that we want to focus on the topic of fairness for the next few days. Students are given a supply of Post-its and are asked to go back and find some parts in the story that add credence to their ideas concerning the topic of fairness. One student gets a large sheet of chart paper and writes down some of the ideas discussed in the group today. This chart will help us keep a visual "trail" of our thinking and the issues that have arisen in our discussion.

After meeting with the lit group, I am scheduled to work with another group of children in what I call a "strategy group." I gather together five or six students from around the room for a short meeting. After close observation of my students, I have decided that these students need some help using context clues in their reading. It seems that they overrely on the "sound-it-out" strategy as a primary strategy during their reading. I have decided to use a "cloze" procedure, where I take a text and intentionally cover some specific words to see what strategies they will use to predict the covered words. We meet for about fifteen minutes and discuss our strategies for predicting the covered words, and then I ask students to try these strategies the next time they are reading on their own and tell me how it works. I will meet with them again next week to check on their progress.

I walk over to the tape player and put on some soft jazz music. This is the signal for students to take a few minutes and write down the names of the books they have been reading in their reading logs. These logs are a simple form that I created for students to keep track of all the various books and materials they read during the year. It has columns for the date, the title of the book, the number of pages, and a small section for comments. By the end of the year, these logs are filled with literally hundreds of books that children have been exposed to during the reading workshop.

Within a few minutes, children begin to gather on the rug for our "sharing circle." At the end of every reading workshop, we gather together to share our ideas or concerns about our reading or the workshop itself. Three girls eagerly share their ideas about a new book they are reading together called *Absolutely Normal Chaos*. This is another book by Sharon Creech, author of the Newbery-winning book *Walk Two Moons*, which I had just finished reading to the class last week. In this new book, the character Mary Lou Finney is one of the characters that we met in *Walk Two Moons*, and they are excited to follow along with more of her adventures.

Some students share new titles they have found, while others remain silent, listening to the comments of their peers. One boy shares a new reading strategy that he learned at home with his father. He realized that in the index of a nonfiction book, the page numbers listed in bold print are pages with illustrations. This has helped him with his inquiry project focusing on the Grand Canyon. We talk about this for a minute, look at a nonfiction book from the classroom library as an example, and decide as a group that this is an important strategy that should be added to our reading strategies chart. I tell him to add it to the list on the wall when he has the time.

It is time for us to go to art class, so I ask the students to gather near the door, and off we go.

What Just Happened?

I would consider this a rather typical day in the life of our reading workshop. Although reading aloud and reading demonstrations take place throughout the day, the reading workshop is a single block of time dedicated to the exploration of literature and the development of children's reading processes. Whether we are discussing the different types of illustrations in selected picture books or appreciating the beautiful language in a new poem, the reading workshop provides the space and opportunities for children to experience and discuss quality pieces of literature.

To the unaccustomed observer, the reading workshop may look very chaotic, with children doing a variety of things at the same time. However, the reading workshop is not a haphazard jumble of events; rather, it is an active environment where children work independently or in small groups on various projects, deciding what to read, where to sit, and with whom to work. It may look overly busy, but there is an underlying structure that helps children make their own decisions and accept responsibility for their learning. It provides clear expectations for their behavior and the experiences they encounter.

The structure of the reading workshop must be consistent enough to provide support for children's development, yet remain flexible enough to respond to those "teachable moments" that arise in the everyday events of the classroom. A knowledgeable teacher, not the designers of the scope and sequence of a commercially designed reading program, decides what to teach in response to the needs of the children and the resources available.

Before I discuss my theoretical understandings about reading and learning, the guiding principles that inform my instructional practice, and the curricular components that make up the learning experiences I provide in the reading workshop, I want to explain the various events that I described in the opening scene. John Dewey expressed the concern that what is taught today should build upon what was taught previously, and it should lead to what will be taught in the future. I believe that the reading workshop should follow this premise. The experiences of today's reading workshop should build upon the experiences of the previous day's workshop and lead to the new experiences of the coming days. It is important for the reader of this book to understand how a single day's reading workshop is structured and operates, but it is equally important, if not more so, to understand how the reading workshop operates over time.

As I explained, our day begins with pairs of children sharing the entries in their literature response logs that they completed for homework. Each evening, students are expected to read for at least half an hour and to write an entry in their response logs. These logs are a notebook that children use to record their impressions, connections, and wonderings about their readings. The format of these literature response logs will be discussed in Chapter 9, "Evaluations."

After about fifteen minutes, I start a song on the cassette player in my room to signal to students to put things away and gather on the floor in the front of the room to begin our day. I use a song that gives students enough time to put things away, which gradually fades out so that they know when we are ready to begin our "opening ceremonies." I have found that using particular songs for the transitions between classroom events allows children to monitor their time and be ready when we are ready to start, without a word from the teacher.

These opening ceremonies are a ritual that occurs each and every morning. They serve as a consistent way to talk to each other, share the events and experiences of our lives, and get off to a great start for the day. I have found that beginning the day by sharing the special events in our lives allows us to get to know and respect each other as members of our learning community. This form of "show and tell," or community share, is an important time for students to be recognized. It is also a time for me to learn more about them. I have learned a great deal from the interesting stories my students have told, and this time provides an opportunity for children to practice their oral language skills.

After we share our experiences in this "community circle," I begin the reading workshop by reading a picture book aloud to the group every day. The books that I read are not selected at random; rather, I choose books that are connected by similar theme, genre, author, or content topics. The reading aloud of picture books, poems, chapter books, and nonfiction materials anchors the sounds of language in children; builds community; introduces new authors, genres, and titles; and provides an opportunity for children to discuss literature. It is an important part of the reading workshop, and something that I do several times a day, every day. I use picture books in the writing workshop to introduce writing craft, in the math workshop to help explain mathematical concepts, and in our sciences workshop to share content information.

After reading and discussing a particular book or poem, I use a comparison chart or a web chart to create a visual representation of our thinking. These various charts line the walls of our room so we can refer to them as our studies progress, allowing us to make connections across the discussions of different days. I will discuss these charts further in Chapter 6, "Explorations." I feel it is important to keep visual representations of our classroom learning experiences for students to revisit, and to help organize our thinking and our studies.

When the discussion concerning the picture book I have read winds down, I check my schedule to see which children I am meeting with for a reading conference. These conferences are brief, two- to three-minute discussions, where I check on what students have done in the reading workshop for the past week. I make a few notes in my observational record folder for that child and move on to the next child. This is my way of keeping track of individual students' progress, and checking to see if there are any problems with reading that I can help with. I explain these conferences and my observational record-keeping system in Chapter 9, "Evaluations."

After these brief reading conferences, I am usually scheduled to meet with a literature study group, a reading strategy group, or both. I typically work with lit study groups three days a week and reading strategy groups the other two days. These meetings take about fifteen to twenty minutes each, depending on the topic and the discussion. In the reading strategy groups, I have called children together for the purpose of demonstrating an explicit reading strategy using a piece of authentic literature. (I will explain this further in Chapter 8, "Instruction.") In the lit study groups, I am facilitating small group of children's discussion of a particular children's novel. The discussions are designed to help children "dig deeper" into a piece of literature, and to help them make sense of the story by sharing ideas with members of the group and listening to others' perspectives. These groups change as the books children are reading change. I'll say more about literature study groups in Chapter 7, "Investigations."

While I am working with these groups of children, other children are working on various projects, reading independently or in small groups, listening to books on cassette tape, preparing for a lit study presentation, or doing research for our unit of study in math or sciences. Children assume a great deal of responsibility for their learning during the reading workshop. They are expected to have a plan for the workshop and to be able to solve many of their own challenges. This arrangement does not come easily, nor does it evolve without a great deal of patience, time, and practice. By being involved in the planning and procedures of the reading workshop, students learn responsibility for their development as readers and the expectations we have created for our learning community. Chapter 3, "Creating a Space for Readers," addresses how I get to this "level of operation."

At the end of the workshop time, students gather in a circle to share their ideas. Like the author's chair at the end of the writing workshop, this sharing circle serves several purposes. First, it allows children to hear from their peers about new books, authors, and reading strategies. Second, this sharing time adds to our growing sense of community, as we learn to respect and live together throughout the year. Finally, it acts as a "window" for me to assess children's progress and come to understand the challenges and experiences that children are having in the classroom. In actuality, every workshop that we have—writing, math, and sciences—ends with a sharing circle. They allow time for us to reflect on our learning and hear the ideas and opinions of others in the classroom.

Reflections

One of the biggest challenges for me in designing my reading workshop is to create a framework that supports children's development as readers and provides a consistent, predictable environment that allows children to be successful.

Consistency is an important aspect of the reading workshop; however, I don't want our routines to become tedious and uninspiring. The structures I put in place need to free children to be creative, to allow them to read and explore new texts, and to experience the joys of children's literature.

The experiences that I provide in the reading workshop are a blend of "pre-planned engagements" and "response-centered instruction." I don't go into the daily reading workshop unprepared, but I also don't go in unwilling to adapt my plans to address particular needs that may arise. I have experiences planned ahead of time, but these plans are flexible, and I am always ready to change them in response to the needs and interests of my students. The ability to provide learning experiences that support children's development as competent readers, and to respond to the day-to-day interactions in the reading workshop, is a crucial element in creating a successful literature-based reading environment.

2

Why Do I Do What I Do?

*Theory should help us provide the conditions, the contexts that will
foster growth toward competent reading. Most important, theory
should help us to avoid methods and strategies that may satisfy
short-term goals but obstruct growth.*

LOUISE ROSENBLATT

As classroom teachers, we need to be able to plan effective day-to-day experiences
in the reading workshop; however, we must also be able to make decisions about
the learning conditions and curricular components we provide over the course of
the school year. Each of these decisions should be directly related to the knowledge and beliefs we hold about reading and learning, and to the information we
have gathered about our students through the various assessments we use in our
classrooms. In this way, our understandings of the learning and reading processes,
and of the students in our classrooms, drive our instructional practices, the learning environment we establish, and the experiences we provide our students.

In other words, theory should drive practice. However, in order for this to
occur, as classroom teachers we need to "unpack" our beliefs about reading and
learning so that we may critically examine them, and be able to articulate "why we
do what we do" to ourselves and external audiences, such as parents, administrators, or the public in general.

I begin this chapter by explaining the *theoretical understandings* that provide
the foundations for my reading workshop. Based on these understandings, I have
developed a set of *guiding principles* that provide the framework for making decisions about what occurs in the reading workshop. These guiding principles help
me to keep a close connection between my understandings (theories) and my

1. Invitations: Bringing Children and Literature Together
2. Explorations: Coming to Know Literature
3. Investigations: Digging Deeper into Literature
4. Instruction: Facilitating Children's Development as Readers
5. Evaluation: Coming to Know Children as Readers

Figure 2–1. *Curricular Components*

teaching (practice). All of the learning experiences that take place in my class-room are designed with these guiding principles in mind.

These guiding principles govern the ways in which I implement my reading workshop; what's more, they enable me to conceptualize the workshop as five separate yet interrelated *curricular components*, which form the heart and soul of the reading workshop, that include all of the actual learning experiences in my reading workshop (see Figure 2–1). Each of these curricular components will constitute its own separate chapter later in the book.

Theoretical Understandings

Reading is the construction of meaning. It is a two-way process, as readers bring meaning to a text in order to construct meaning with a text. In other words, as Louise Rosenblatt (1978) has written, readers are active participants in the reading process, building their understandings as they "transact" with a text. Different readers may construct different meanings from the same text or experiences, depending upon the knowledge and experiences they bring to the reading event. The goal of the reader is to understand what they have read, to make sense of the text. In order to do this, each individual reader uses their understanding of the world, their knowledge of language, and the relationship between the letters and the sounds of their language to construct meaning, to make sense, as they transact with a text. Reading is not simply the correct identification of individual words, nor is it the ability to read words out loud without mistakes. Reading is understanding what one reads. It is making sense of a text. Any transaction with a text must result in the construction of meaning for it to fit within my definition of reading.

Reading instruction should develop lifelong, active readers. How we transact with texts is largely determined by the experiences and demonstrations we are provided, how reading is taught in schools, and the expectations we are presented with as readers. Some reading programs tend to create passive readers, ones who sit back and wait for the teacher to determine what was important in the text. Unfortunately, passive readers see no direct pleasure in reading and generally do not become lifelong readers because they find no purpose in reading. In our class-rooms, we want children to understand why they are reading, to assume an active stance to the reading process, and to develop as lifelong readers who choose to read throughout their lives for many purposes.

We learn to read by reading. We generally learn to do this in the company of other competent readers. Frank Smith reminded educators of the old adage "You learn from the company you keep" when he wrote about "joining the literacy club." If we want children to become readers, they need to "keep company" with other readers, to see themselves as potential readers, and to experience actual reading events. In essence, children need to identify themselves as readers in order to join the "literacy club."

We must provide large amounts of time for students to interact with liter-ature. As classroom teachers, we need to provide numerous opportunities to read and be read to, access to a wide range of reading materials, and a responsive, car-ing environment that allows children to share their reactions to their readings without fear of humiliation. Reading "instruction" must be a part of this environ-ment, not isolated from it. We don't learn to read by doing skills worksheets, only later to try these skills out on a real book. We learn to read by transacting with authentic literature, for authentic purposes.

People teach people to read, not commercial programs. Authors, teachers, and parents are among the many catalysts that bring children and texts together and show them how to read and how various texts work. It is the skill of the class-room teacher, based on their knowledge of the reading process and the children in their classrooms, that makes the reading workshop successful. Blindly following a teacher's manual or the scope and sequence of a commercial reading program will not help all children become competent readers. Some children will learn to read in spite of the program, and some will fall through the proverbial cracks. It takes a knowledgeable, sensitive, observant teacher to support the efforts of all children, and to help them develop as successful, lifelong readers.

Guiding Principles

Based on my theoretical understandings, I have developed a set of principles for my reading workshop. These principles are 1) opportunity, 2) choice, 3) response, 4) relevance/authenticity, 5) space, 6) faith, and 7) uncertainty. I use these prin-ciples to help me make decisions about the various learning experiences I provide in my reading workshop.

1. **Opportunity:** In order to provide children with the opportunities they need to become successful readers, children need time to read, access to a large variety of quality reading materials, and a classroom structure that supports social interaction. They need time to browse through books and explore what they find. They also need the opportunity to discuss what they read with other readers. In essence, they need to become members of a community of readers.

2. **Choice:** Children need to make choices about what they read, what groups to participate in, and how to respond to their readings. This does not mean, however, that the teacher abdicates all control over the classroom; it just means that teachers involve children in as many decisions as possible. In my reading workshop, we share control, and students become empowered by their extended roles. Nancie Atwell (1987) called this concept "ownership." She believed, as I do, that students need to be part of the decision-making process in order to gain ownership of their learning. When this happens, students begin to assume responsibility for their growth as readers and as members of our reading community.

3. **Response:** Children need response to their efforts. They need to receive feedback about their attempts and encouragement for their achievements. Students not only need to receive responses from the teacher and their peers, they also need the opportunity to respond themselves to the texts they read. During group discussions and literature studies, I want to encourage students to openly share their ideas and concerns, and feel confident in expressing their responses to literature. How we respond to their ideas will greatly affect their continued engagement in these classroom experiences.

4. **Relevance/Authenticity:** The experiences that we provide in our classrooms must have a close relationship to the events in the actual world outside of schools. We need to be careful that the things we do in school aren't just designed to make us better at school, but better at reading, writing, mathematics, and other things outside of school. The closer this relationship, the more relevant and authentic the experiences.

5. **Space:** Children need a supportive environment in which to develop as readers. Whether this means creating a safe place to make mistakes or allowing children the extra time they need to develop, they need space. This space has physical and psychological aspects to it. Children need the physical space to be comfortable as they read, but also the psychological space to try out new ideas without fear of reprisal. The design of our workshop should not restrict opportunities; rather, it should create

space for children to interact with caring, supportive teachers and peers in a learning community.

6. **Faith:** We need to have faith in our children as "makers of meaning," and ourselves as "responders" to their efforts. Much of education today is based on accountability, which is in actuality lack of faith in teachers, parents, and students. If we believed that given the opportunity children will learn and teachers will teach, the educational environment would be radically different. When we sit with lit study groups or finish a read aloud, if we have chosen a book that connects to our children, we need to have faith that they will respond and react to the story. When we quickly jump in and start asking questions, we are not showing faith in our students. When principals and school districts quickly jump in and buy commercial programs that teachers must obediently follow, they are not showing much faith in us as professionals. Like all faiths, this one involves trust and confidence in ourselves and others. As teachers, can we really think about our children any other way?

7. **Uncertainty:** Reading is a highly complex event that cannot be reduced to a formula or a commercial program. As teachers, we need to be able to live with a certain amount of uncertainty as we work with developing readers. Assessments give us a limited "window" into students' abilities and needs, and at times we may become stumped about which course of action to take with individual readers. If reading were a simple "diagnose-prescribe" or "assess-then-teach" relationship, programs alone would be able to teach all readers to read in a relatively short period of time. As classroom teachers, we know that this is not the case. We must become "reflective practitioners" who continually question our practice, keep an open mind about the methods and experiences we provide in our classrooms, and use assessments to inquire into the needs, interests, and abilities of our students. However, with this stance of "reflective practitioner" comes a certain amount of uncertainty. We need to be able to act on our beliefs without allowing those beliefs to close our minds to new possibilities. In essence, we have to be able to act, while at the same time critiquing our actions.

Five Curricular Components

Five separate yet interrelated curricular components form the core of my reading workshop and offer a comprehensive, balanced approach to reading instruction. These components are:

1. **Invitations: Bringing Children and Literature Together:** By reading aloud to children and providing access to a wide variety of quality works of literature, nonfiction, poetry, and other materials, we invite children into the world of reading. As classroom teachers, it is our job to extend multiple invitations for children to sample, explore, and become involved with different reading materials. We need to create an environment that provides the opportunity for literature and children to come together, and successfully invite them to join our literate community.

2. **Explorations: Coming to Know Literature:** Children need support in moving past the "I liked the book" phase, in order to make more sophisticated connections to texts. We need to provide experiences that help children explore the various elements and structures of literature. By focusing on particular books, authors, themes, and content topics, we help children make deeper, more meaningful connections to literature. As designers and facilitators of the reading workshop, we are trying to provide experiences that help children see new patterns and relationships in the literature that we are exploring.

3. **Investigations: Digging Deeper into Literature:** We want children to "dig deeper" into the literature they read. The primary means for doing this in my reading workshop is through literature study groups. By helping children develop a "passionate attention" for the literature they read, and by providing the opportunity for them to share their reactions to their readings with other students in collaborative study groups, we help children dig beneath the surface layers of literature to uncover the more complex patterns and meanings possible in quality works of literature.

4. **Instruction: Facilitating Children's Development as Readers:** In the reading workshop, teachers work hard to help children learn how to read. We don't simply abandon them to wander aimlessly among our classroom libraries! By using various grouping strategies, sharing a wealth of reading materials, and teaching a range of reading strategies, I carefully guide the development of my students as successful readers. In my reading workshop, teaching is direct and explicit; it focuses on the development of reading strategies in the context of authentic reading events.

5. **Evaluation: Coming to Know Children as Readers:** My decisions about what to teach and when to teach it are based primarily on my close observation and continuous classroom-based evaluation of the children. Using a variety of assessment procedures, or "windows," we teachers begin to develop a better understanding of the children in our

classrooms. We can then use this understanding to make decisions about the resources, experiences, and learning environments that we provide for our students. I will share several of the assessment "windows" that I have found helpful in coming to know the readers in my classrooms.

These curricular components operate over time to provide the learning experiences in my reading workshop and provide a consistent and effective structure for our learning environment. This book is designed to help teachers see the "big picture" of the reading workshop, as well as the specific details of my daily instructional practice.

Reflections

Literature is more than a resource used to teach children how to read. Literature is also one of the major reasons to become literate. One of the major concerns I have about writing a book about teaching reading in a literature-based classroom is that the primary focus is then on the teaching of reading, and the secondary focus is on the literature itself.

In my reading workshop, literature is the central resource to help children learn how to read, but it does so much more than that. Literature illuminates life. It brings meaning to our human existence and helps us deal with the world in which we live. Reading literature is an end in itself, not merely a vehicle for becoming a competent "decoder."

Literature is based on story, and so is much of the way we live and understand our lives. We are introduced to stories as young children, and come to understand ourselves, others, and our relationships to other people by the stories we hear and tell. Ralph Peterson and Maryann Eeds, two of my mentors during my undergraduate studies, say that story is an exploration and illumination of life. As readers, we live within the story world, and because of this we have access to insights, experiences, and perceptions that would otherwise not be available.

Literature is an authentic text written to tell a story, not to teach the "short a" vowel sound. We read literature to enter the world the author creates, and to follow along with the characters we have come to know and love. We empathize with them, cry with them, and chase their dreams. Without literature there would be little, if any, reason to learn to read in the first place.

The reading workshop is situated among many other workshop-like blocks of time, where I support children's development as writers, mathematicians, scientists, and citizens in a democracy. It is a way of organizing educational experiences that has worked for me for many years. Let's now discuss the social interactions as well as the physical arrangements that make up my classroom learning environment.

Further Readings

CAMBOURNE, BRIAN. 1988. *The Whole Story: Natural Learning and the Acquisition of Literacy*. Auckland, New Zealand: Scholastic.

CLAY, MARIE. 1991. *Becoming Literate: The Construction of Inner Control*. Portsmouth, NH: Heinemann.

GOODMAN, KENNETH S. 1996. *On Reading*. Portsmouth, NH: Heinemann.

ROSENBLATT, L. 1978. *The Reader, the Text, the Poem: The Transactional Theory of the Literary Work*. Carbondale, IL: Southern Illinois University Press.

SMITH, FRANK. 1988. *Joining the Literacy Club*. Portsmouth, NH: Heinemann.

WEAVER, CONSTANCE. 1994. *Reading Process and Practice: From Socio-Psycholinguistics to Whole Language*. Second Edition. Portsmouth, NH: Heinemann.

3

Creating a Space for Readers

Adding a focus on literature to the curriculum will result in only small changes in readers' talk about books unless there is also a fundamental change in the social relationships within the classroom.

KATHY SHORT

Over the past several years, I have found myself spending more and more time, and money, at the large retail bookstore around the corner from my home. Early on Saturday mornings, before the store fills up with people, I wander around the store browsing through the current periodicals, *New York Times* bestsellers, photography books, and travel guides. Some Saturdays, I have a particular title in mind, other times I am simply there to see what new books are available. Rarely, if ever, do I leave the store empty-handed.

The bookstore near my home has gone to great lengths to ensure that their store is a comfortable place to spend time. A bakery located in the back of the store serves croissants, pastries, cappuccino, and other special coffees and baked delicacies. Soft jazz music playing in the background lends to the relaxed atmosphere throughout the store. There are nice comfortable chairs and sofas to relax on while looking through various books and magazines. No one pressures you while you are there, yet the sales assistants are available if you should ever need assistance. These amenities have been designed with the reader, in this case also the customer, in mind. These stores are designed to make the customer feel comfortable, provide access to a large variety of books and magazines, and to invite customers to wander around, take their time, and choose books and magazines to buy.

Inevitably, I am drawn to the children's literature section of the store. The colorful chairs, the posters hanging on the walls, and the enormous selection of children's literature entice me to find a comfortable chair and browse through new titles or reread some old favorites. This section of the store reminds me of where I sit and read when I am at home. Sitting in the comfortable chair in my office or relaxing on my living room sofa, I am surrounded by different books to suit my various moods and interests. At home, or in this bookstore, I can take advantage of extended blocks of time and a comfortable chair to read in without being interrupted.

At this bookstore, as at my home, there is no pressure to make a quick selection. No one is forcing me to choose a book immediately or hurrying me along. In fact, I rarely go to this bookstore when I am rushed or have a short amount of time. I like to go there and spend time browsing through what is available. The store is designed for people to wander around and browse through the available titles, not to be hurried along. The store designers and managers know that the longer I spend time looking, the more likely I am to make a purchase.

Unfortunately, in many schools children are given limited time and opportunities to browse through the library collection, choose a book, and find a comfortable place to read for extended blocks of time. Shortened library periods force children to hurry up and make a book selection or run the risk of forfeiting their opportunity to pick out a book until the following week. Sustained Silent Reading (SSR) times are usually ten to fifteen minutes long and require all children and teachers to drop what they are doing and read. Classrooms are coming to resemble assembly lines, where children move along a conveyor belt while the teacher drops information into them in thirty- or forty-minute time blocks.

As classroom teachers, we need to provide extended amounts of time on a daily basis for reading; however, I feel that this block of time alone is not sufficient. I would also like to see schools and individual classrooms take a lesson from retail bookstores like those I have described. In these bookstores, the sales clerks are available, but not imposing. Helpful, but not pushy. The atmosphere is relaxed and inviting. The physical space is comfortable and aesthetically pleasing, providing access to a wealth of reading materials and time to enjoy one's selections. Even though there is little or no pressure from the sales clerks to purchase any books, I can't remember a time when I left the store empty-handed. The question, it seems, is whether we are providing the same opportunities in our classrooms for our students that the bookstores are providing for its customers.

We can learn a few new things from these store managers, sales clerks, and bookstore designers. Our classrooms, and especially our classroom "library corners," need to be inviting places, where students rarely, if ever, leave without making a selection. Like the displays and reading areas in retail bookstores, the elementary classroom should provide access to a wide range of reading materials, a comfortable place to relax and read, extended periods of time for children to engage in their reading, a teacher who knows about children's literature and reading processes to support children's development as readers, and numerous opportunities for students to interact with other readers. As teachers, we should be available, but not imposing. Helpful, but not pushy. To us falls the task of inviting, not coercing, children into the world of reading and literature.

In this chapter, I will discuss how I begin each year by involving children in the design and arrangement of the physical environment of the classroom. Early in the year, we focus on the creation and maintenance of the classroom library and the various "spaces" we need to create in the room for us to work and share ideas. During the beginning weeks of school, I am trying to create a community of readers, a place where readers read and share their reactions to their reading with other readers. I pay particular attention to how the social dimensions of our classroom evolve and how the students and I create the classroom expectations and routines for the various parts of our day. As the opening quote from Kathy Short suggests, until we closely examine the social relationships and interactions (and I would add the physical dimensions of the learning environment), we will not change the way that teachers and students talk about literature and develop as members of a community of readers.

Creating a Community of Readers

As children enter the classroom on the first day of the school year, the walls of the room are empty, the tables and chairs are placed in a temporary arrangement, and the library books are stacked in boxes in one corner of the room. There are shelves, couches, book racks, easels, filing cabinets, planters, and a stereo set along the perimeter of the room. As students enter the room, I invite them to come over and sit down on the carpet near my rocking chair, located in the front of the room. We introduce ourselves to each other, and students usually share the postcards that they received at home from me before school began. I always send a postcard to my prospective students before school begins, introducing myself and inviting them to come and join our learning community. In a sense, our community begins before my students even enter the classroom.

I begin by explaining that we will be designing the room together, arranging the furniture to meet our needs. I make sure to tell them that it's not because I was lazy that the room didn't get arranged; rather, it is because I believe that we need to work together to design the room. I talk to them about the special areas that we will need to create—for example, the classroom library, the group discussion area, the "work area," the students' cubbies, a place for art supplies, a publishing center, and a classroom museum (see Figure 3–1). Some of the first decisions we will have to make will be to decide how the room will be arranged, where

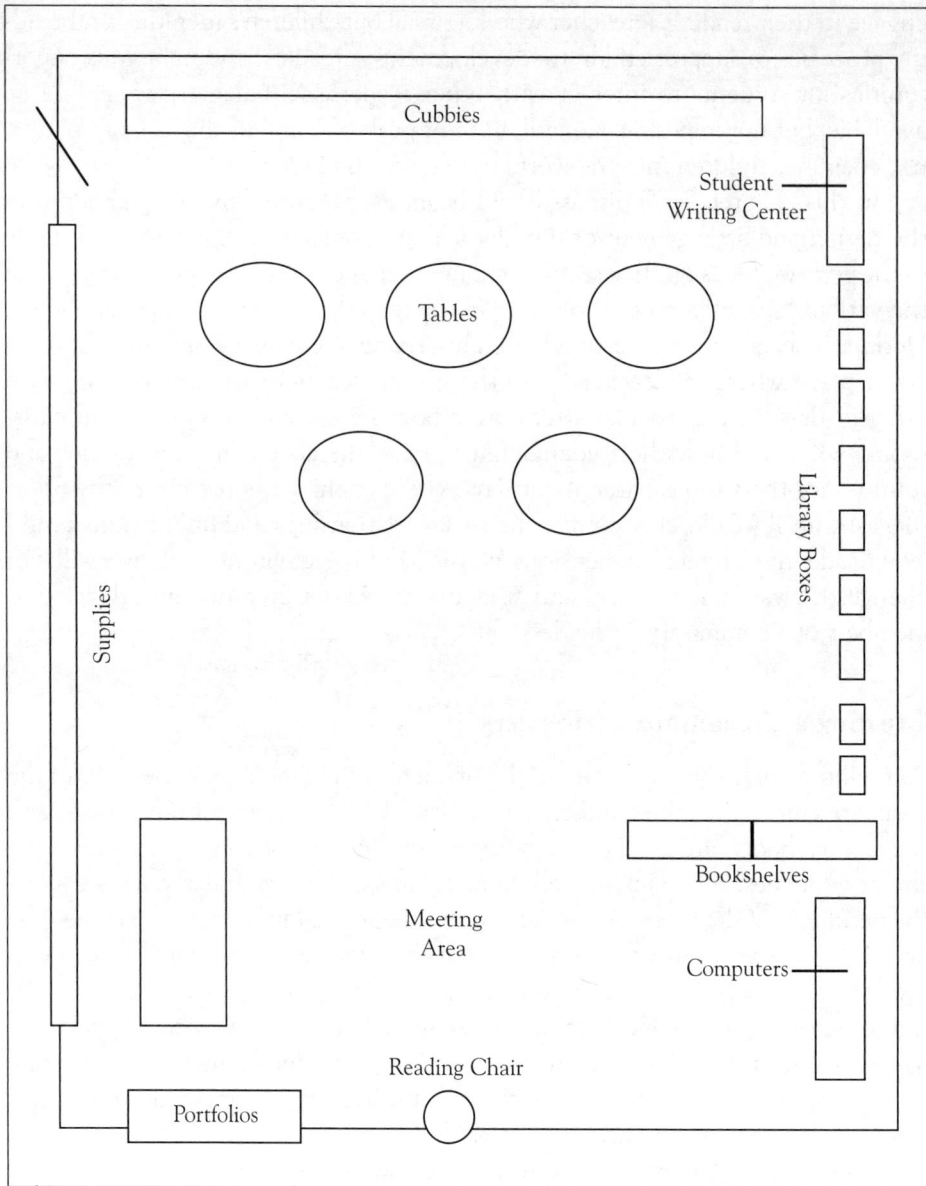

Figure 3–1. *Classroom Diagram*

the library will go, where the furniture will be placed, and how the children
will organize the art supplies and other materials they will use all year long. We will
have to decide what jobs will be needed and who will be assigned to them. We
will need students to volunteer to work in groups to design and organize specific

parts of the room. For the first few days, this creation of our physical space, and the jobs and routines needed to keep it functioning, will be our main focus.

Behind the rocking chair that I use for reading aloud with the class, there is a large colorful sign that reads "Living Together Differently." As our introductions finish up, I direct students' attention to this sign. It's not hard to miss since it's one of the only things hanging on the wall. I ask students what they think this saying means, and we talk about these words and how they might affect our time together. I explain to them that I hope this motto can help guide our actions and the ways in which we treat each other throughout the whole year and beyond. We spend a great deal of time discussing what this motto means to us and its implications for our classroom community, especially during the beginning of the year. As the year progresses and our community evolves, we will refer back to this motto and its implications for our behaviors and social interactions. For me, this saying is the driving force behind my conception of a learning community.

After this initial discussion, I begin the day as I will for the rest of the year, by reading a story to the class. For me, one of the most important factors in the building of our classroom community comes from the sharing of ideas and reactions to a piece of literature. I begin the year reading from a collection of books that address the issue of diversity and what it means to be different (see Figure 3–2). These books also invite discussions concerning what it means to be an individual, what it feels like to be different, and what it is like to be a member of a community of learners. The discussions that we have about these books help children understand the issues and challenges that arise in living together differently.

BABBITT, NATALIE. 1996. *Bub, Or the Very Best Thing*. New York: HarperCollins.

BAYLOR, BYRD. 1993. *The Table Where Rich People Sit*. New York: Greenwillow.

BROWNE, ANTHONY. 1989. *Willy the Wimp*. Albuquerque, NM: Dragonfly Books.

———. 1990. *Piggybook*. New York: Knopf.

COONEY, BARBARA. 1985. *Miss Rumphius: Story and Pictures*. New York: Viking Press.

EVERITT, BETSY. 1995. *Mean Soup*. New York: Voyager.

FOX, MEM. 1997. *The Straight Line Wonder*. Greenvale, NY: Mondo.

———. 1989. *Koala Lou*. San Diego, CA: Harcourt Brace.

Figure 3–2. *Books About Building Community*

GIFF, PATRICIA REILLY. 1984. *Today Was a Terrible Day*. New York: Viking Press.

GOSS, LINDA. 1996. *The Frog Who Wanted to Be a Singer*. New York: Orchard Books.

HENKES, KEVIN. 1993. *Owen*. New York: Greenwillow.

———. 1996. *Chrysanthemum*. New York: Mulberry Books.

———. 1996. *Lilly's Purple Plastic Purse*. New York: Greenwillow.

HOWE, JAMES. 1999. *Horace and Morris, but Mostly Dolores*. New York: Atheneum.

KNOWLES, SHEENA. 1998. *Edward the Emu*. New York: HarperCollins.

KRAUS, ROBERT. 1998. *Leo the Late Bloomer*. New York: HarperCollins Juvenile.

KRAUSS, RUTH. 1993. *The Carrot Seed*. New York: Harperfestival.

LESTER, HELEN. 1988. *Tacky the Penguin*. Boston: Houghton Mifflin.

LIONNI, LEO. 1990. *Frederick*. New York: Knopf.

———. 1992. *Swimmy*. New York: Knopf.

LITTLE, JEAN. 1990. *Hey World, Here I Am!* New York: HarperCollins.

PINKWATER, DANIEL. 1977. *The Big Orange Splot*. New York: Hastings House.

RASCHKA, CHRISTOPHER. 1993. *Yo! Yes?* New York: Orchard Books.

ROSEN, MICHAEL. 1996. *This Is Our House*. Cambridge, MA: Candlewick Press.

SEUSS, DR., JACK PRELUTSKY, AND LANE SMITH. 1998. *Hooray for Diffendoofer Day!* New York: Knopf.

SMITH, LANE. 1991. *Glasses, Who Needs 'Em?* New York: Viking Press.

THOMAS, VALERIE. 1990. *Winnie the Witch*. Brooklyn, NY: Kane/Miller.

VIORST, JUDITH. 1984. *If I Were in Charge of the World and Other Worries*. New York: Aladdin Paperbacks.

———. 1987. *Alexander and the Terrible, Horrible, No Good, Very Bad Day*. New York: Aladdin Paperbacks.

WHITCOMB, MARY. 1998. *Odd Velvet*. San Francisco, CA: Chronicle Books.

WOOD, AUDREY. 1996. *Elbert's Bad Word*. San Diego, CA: Harcourt Brace.

Figure 3–2. *Books About Building Community (continued)*

I begin the year, as I have done for my many years of teaching, by reading the picture book *Tacky the Penguin*, by Helen Lester, and the first chapter of *Dominic*, by William Steig. *Tacky the Penguin* deals with the issue of being different and an individual, while *Dominic* talks about making decisions about what road to take in life. The character Dominic is confronted by a split in the road during his journey. As he is wondering which way to go, an alligator witch explains that one road leads to daydreaming and boredom, while the other is the "road to adventure." These are the messages I want to begin the year discussing with my students: being an individual and making good choices. Of course, many other things always arise in our discussions, but these are certainly a major part of the first discussion circles.

We continue with our discussion by creating a chart about our ideas concerning the motto on the board and the two books we have read. I have a large piece of butcher paper that I roll out on another part of the wall, and we use this to write down our ideas about community. I write the words "Living Together Differently" along the top of the chart, and we add our ideas that we have discussed to it. This chart will grow as we read new books over the course of the next few weeks. Each new book will bring a different perspective to the discussion about community and the concept of living together differently. It is an important discussion to begin with, and one that I feel is worth the time and effort because of the positive effects it can have on the rest of the school year.

After the opening discussion focusing on these two books, I share with my students the expectations that I have for the classroom community. They are simply:

1. Think
2. Say What You Think (in an appropriate manner)
3. Include Everyone
4. Enjoy Yourselves
5. Practice Kindness
6. Do Your Best

It is my hope that these expectations, along with the class motto, will set the tone for our classroom community. Any other rules or procedures that need to be made will be made together. If students know in their hearts and in their minds that we as teachers take them and their ideas seriously, they will be more willing to share their ideas and concerns. We discuss my list of expectations and what they mean to us, and then go play kickball. I believe that we develop community by sharing in events, both inside and outside the classroom. I like to plan a field trip early in the first month of school, usually to the public library to get library cards, to help build this sense of community. We play together, learn together, and live together. That is at the heart of our development as a community of readers and learners.

The Physical Dimensions of the Learning Environment

Traditionally, classrooms have been arranged with children seated at individual desks, row after row, facing the teacher's desk at the front of the room, in order to facilitate lectures or direct instructional practices. Supplies, books, and other classroom resources are located on shelves or behind cabinet doors along the perimeter of the room. The room is designed for little or no student-to-student interaction. This "all-desks-in-a-row" arrangement has traditionally been used to direct students to interact exclusively with the teacher in the front of the room. As long as the teacher is viewed as the dispenser of information, standing in front of the class in order to effectively dole out knowledge, this arrangement makes some sense. However, when classroom instruction becomes more child-centered, focusing on the social interactions among students, the physical arrangement needs to change to support these new interactions.

I would like to offer ten ideas for you to consider when designing the physical arrangement of your classroom: "Serafini's Top Ten List of Physical Environment Ideas." Along with each suggestion, I will provide an example from my classroom to help you envision the ideas I present. I am making this list for my "ideal" classroom, the one I design in my dreams. Of course, we have to live in the real world, with real budgets and real restrictions, and we have to adhere to more regulations and directives than we would like to admit. Some of these things are not physical as much as they are conceptual, but this list represents the things I hope to include in my elementary classroom learning environment. Number . . .

10. *Physically Defined Spaces*

By physically arranging furniture to define spaces, such as the class library or reading area, students become aware of the expectations for a particular place in the room. In my classroom, I usually arrange several couches, assorted lamps, and a rug in one part of the room that becomes the reading area. Students seem to enjoy the comfortable surroundings, and this area often becomes a favorite place for children to sit and read. By physically defining the reading area with the furniture, shelves, and rug, I can help students understand what is expected of them when they enter this space.

I use bookshelves and cardboard display cases, along with signs and book boxes, to define the library area. The library is a place to browse through books and make selections. When students are in the library area, this is what is expected of them. (Unfortunately, due to the lack of classroom space, students often don't have enough room in this area to sit and read and still have enough space for students to get around them and make their selections. So much of these expectations are controlled by the amount of space and the arrangement of our classroom furniture.)

9. *Authenticity*

I feel that the classroom should not look like a place that only exists in schools. The room should remind children of home and other places outside of school where people gather. Because of this principle, I invite students to bring in posters, stuffed animals, and other items from home to decorate our room. This makes the classroom a place where children and teachers alike feel at home. Too often, traditional classrooms have a sterile, laboratory atmosphere that resembles a place where no one would want to spend time.

I also believe that music plays an important part in the learning environment. I prefer to have some soft jazz music playing whenever possible to create a soothing atmosphere for readers. Because I dislike fluorescent lighting, I bring in lamps and other incandescent lights to illuminate the room. Many teachers bring in pets, plants, terrariums, and aquariums to brighten up the classroom atmosphere. These things all bring life and experiences from outside the school into the classroom. When the classroom looks like a place that you would choose to spend time, your students will be more comfortable and enjoy spending time there as well.

8. *Group Meeting Area*

In one corner of my room, I always create a place where my students and I can gather together to listen to stories, conduct class meetings, and have whole-group discussions. I generally have one comfortable, special chair in this area that serves many different functions, such as author's chair, read aloud chair, and a place for guests and me to talk to the class. I often use a large piece of carpet to identify the space we use for these group meetings. The rug itself helps to define the floor space and supports our classroom expectations for these group meetings. The meeting area serves as a place to come together to share our ideas, stories, and experiences.

7. *Round Tables with Chairs*

We all have to deal with what we are given to use in our classrooms, but the items I couldn't do without are round tables and chairs. To me there is something distinctive about sitting and working at round tables as compared to rectangular ones or individual desks. At round tables everyone can see everyone else, there is no head of the table, everyone has an equal position, and there is plenty of room to spread out our work. For me, desks are too small and confining for the work we do in schools.

6. *Cubbies or Lockers*

When the classroom has tables and chairs instead of desks, students need a place to put their personal belongings. Cubbies are one way to do this that don't take up too much space, but I prefer ones with doors on them. It helps students feel they have more privacy in the room for their personal things.

5. Hidden Teacher Area

When you walk into a classroom, the first thing you see should not be a huge teacher's desk in the front of the room standing guard over the rest of the classroom. This traditional arrangement of the room demonstrates that the teacher is in complete control and is the focus of all the attention. Student desks are then lined up to face the teacher's desk, so the teacher can keep an eye on everyone. I prefer to have my belongings fade away into the background of the room. I hope that when a visitor comes into my classroom, the first thing they notice is the students and their work, and I hope that I am often a little hard to find because I am on the floor working with my students. I have a private place for my things, I just don't allow it to take up half of the room.

4. Classroom "Museum"

I believe that a room should reflect the topic being studied and that when a visitor enters a classroom, they should be able to tell what is happening in the curriculum. If our class has been involved in a study of the Grand Canyon, there should be maps, posters, artifacts, rocks, photographs, and travel brochures of the Grand Canyon displayed and readily available. One important space in my room that I have facilitated over the past several years is the classroom "museum." Usually starting out as an empty table and some wall space directly above the table, this space is transformed into a museum focusing on the current topic being studied. For our Grand Canyon inquiry project, the table was covered with rocks, travel brochures, topographic trail maps, aerial photographs of the canyon, scenic photography books, and other artifacts that my students and I brought in to display. Each item on the table was accompanied by an index card describing the artifact, listing the name of the donor, and explaining the relationship the artifact had with our study of Grand Canyon.

As the museum grows, we select curators to organize and maintain the collection, and eventually as a class, we develop a museum guide or brochure for visitors to use when touring the museum. The displays and artifacts contained in our museum leave no doubt in a classroom visitor's mind about the content of our current inquiry project.

3. Supply Area

Students need easy access to the materials and supplies in the classroom, and they should not have to ask the teacher in order to get to many of these supplies.

I believe that students take better care of classroom supplies if they are put in charge of the organization and care of them. Putting the supplies in clearly marked containers, teaching children how to care for supplies, and showing them how to order supplies when they are gone helps students accept responsibility for our materials.

2. Publishing Center

The more books students publish, the more books will be available for students to read. The connection between reading and writing is inseparable. We read what we write and write like what we read. If the writing workshop has a successful publishing component, the books created become some of the most frequently read books in the classroom.

Supplies like contact paper, staplers, special stationery, paper fasteners, binding materials, wallpaper, markers, art supplies, and other materials can be included in this area. The more authentic we can make the publishing materials, the more authentic the books will look. This plays an important part in helping students feel like real authors.

1. Student Ideas

And the number one principle of physical design and classroom learning environments is . . . including students in the design of the room and the decisions about the day-to-day operations of the class. This is something that you can't plan ahead for, but it needs to be included in order to make students feel part of the classroom community. It is important to ask students about their ideas for the classroom, what they think would make the room work better, what they would like to do, and what supplies they should have. I feel that students should have the opportunity, through class meetings and other avenues, to suggest ideas for the physical as well as the social environment of the classroom. If we take students' suggestions seriously and include them in the decision-making process, students become more intimately involved in the events in the classroom community, and accept more responsibility for the classroom and their behaviors.

I think closely about these ten ideas as I begin arranging the classroom and developing classroom procedures each school year. Involving students in as many decisions as possible is central to my efforts in building community. Because we develop many of these procedures together and children share in many of the classroom decisions, the classroom belongs to my students and me. It is our room, not mine alone.

The Classroom Library

One of the biggest physical design decisions we will have to make at the beginning of the year is where to put the classroom library and how to arrange it. The library will serve as a central focus for our community of readers, and it must be not only functional, but aesthetically pleasing as well. The design of the classroom library should invite students to browse through the reading materials, make locating a particular title quick and easy, allow students to keep books in some consistent arrangement, and provide a comfortable space for them to select literature to read.

When I began teaching elementary school years ago, one of my deepest concerns was the limited amount of children's literature I had in my classroom. Because of this concern, I quickly became friends with the school librarian and the librarian at the local public library, checking out my limit of books every two weeks in order to have more books for my classroom. At the beginning of the year, I started sending home order sheets for the Lucky Book Club to provide students with the opportunity to buy books for their own collection and to make funds available to increase the number of books in our classroom. I searched through garage and yard sales, used bookstores, and special closeout sales at retail stores, looking for quality literature at discount prices. I also solicited donations from various sources, including my own school district, to help build my classroom collection. I feel that it is crucial to have a large collection of quality literature, ranging in levels of sophistication, to support the different interests and reading abilities in my classroom.

As I mentioned earlier, at the beginning of the year my classroom library is packed away in boxes, stacked into a corner of the room, just waiting to be discovered. Along with these boxes of books are various shelves, wall displays, cardboard display cases, and other organizing materials and pieces of furniture for the children to use when setting up our library. However, there is a reason why these boxes of books, and other classroom materials, are left stacked along the perimeter of the room. Together, the children and I will arrange our classroom, especially the classroom library. We will make the decisions as to how the library will be designed, where the books will go, and what the procedures for the library and classroom will be. I believe that the more students are involved in the creation and maintenance of the classroom library, the more they will use and take care of it.

Unpacking the Classroom Library

In much the same way as Joanne Hindley described in her book *In the Company of Children* (1996), I open one or two boxes of books each day during the first few weeks of school. It takes about that long to open all of the boxes of books

Classroom Library at Beginning of the Year

I now have available. Each day brings a new adventure as we open up a new box to find out what books are inside, what literary treasures await us. This opening of the library boxes is a yearly ritual in my classroom and is designed to help students get a sense of the variety of books that are available. I also do this to help students understand that the books are there for them to read and are not there merely for display purposes. The books in the classroom are there to be looked at, thumbed through, and read. Every book is available to everyone.

As we open each new box, we place the contents on tables around the room to allow students in small groups to spend time investigating each title. We stop periodically to share favorite books we know and love as a whole class, and introduce each other to new titles we haven't seen before. We get excited sharing the books we remember from previous years, as well as any new titles I may have purchased over the summer. Old favorites and new books are strewn across the tabletops, the conversation is lively, and children are beginning to feel like a part of our community of readers. Students use their writers' notebooks to write down any special titles that they want to be sure to revisit soon. I also ask students to write down any categories or genres that they are noticing. I want them to begin to think about ways to organize the books in the library. This organization will be our next class project.

As students are going through the books scattered around on the tables in the classroom, we begin to make a chart of all the types of books or genres that we are finding. Using a large piece of butcher paper, I list all of the names they give to the books in the room. Art books, nature books, funny books, books about friendship, poetry books, fairy tales, counting books, alphabet books, and family stories are just some of the names students have given in the past. After we go through all of the boxes and have listed all the types of books we have found, I take each name and make a separate card for it. This way, we can move them around so we can begin to develop categories based on the common features in the names we have selected. For example, nature books, rock books, space books, and geography books are categorized into a group called "Science Books." This category then becomes one of the shelves or one of the boxes in our library. We have worked together to organize our library, and in the process we have had some great discussions about genres and categories of books.

Of course, there are some books that I keep "hidden away" for surprises during the year, but for the most part all of my books are available to my students from the beginning of the school year. I do keep some extremely valuable books and some autographed copies of certain titles on a special shelf near my desk, but these are also available for students to read—they simply have to ask. I want students to feel free to select any books in the classroom, while at the same time I teach them to assume responsibility for caring for the classroom book collection.

As the various boxes are opened during the beginning of the year, small groups of children assume responsibility for the creation of the library, the checkout procedures, the signs and posters for the library walls, the arrangement of the library furniture, the plants that will decorate the library, and any other library jobs that we decide are important. We decide together what jobs are needed and what routines and procedures should be created. I feel that any jobs or procedures that students can handle by themselves, without teacher involvement, should be given over to the students as soon as possible. The more students are involved, the more books will be handled, read, and cared for. Eventually, everyone in the class is assigned a job. In this way, I hope to make each child feel like an important part of our community.

Displaying Books

Although there is a central library area for a majority of the books to be housed in the classroom, books are also displayed throughout the room. For example, books about weather are located near the windows along with selections of nature poems, while books about plants and insects are placed near our terrarium. Various titles, displayed in colorful book boxes, are arranged by author, topic, and theme throughout the room for easy access and organization. Some boxes are filled with

Dr. Seuss books, while others may be filled with books about rocks and minerals for our geology study. During the year we have long discussions about the organization of these books and the contents of the various book boxes. The discussions that these organizational efforts inspire are excellent opportunities to discuss the concept of genre and the distinctions between narrative and expository texts.

In many supermarkets, end-of-the-aisle displays, along with other point-of-sale displays near the checkout aisle, are used to draw attention to various products. We can use these same marketing techniques in our classrooms to draw attention to particular titles, genres of books, and authors. Books that are displayed with the covers facing the students tend to get selected more often than books where only the spine is showing. The graphics and artwork on the covers of new books are marketing tools in and of themselves. By creating aesthetically pleasing visual displays and providing easy access to a large variety of books, we are able to entice children into discovering new titles, authors, and genres.

One idea I have used in our library to display picture books is to buy some metal rain gutters to hang along the wall. You can purchase these rain gutters quite cheaply from one of the large retail home improvement stores. They hold a large number of books, are easily mounted on the walls, and provide a nice display of the covers of various picture books. They are also easy to store and rehang each year.

Classroom Library During the Year

Classroom Library During the Year

Checking Out Books

Over the course of the year, my students and I develop a checkout procedure for the books in the classroom library. The structure of the classroom library should be simple enough so that children can take charge of the procedures for checking books in and out, arranging the collection, and adding new titles throughout the year. The library should be designed to respond to the changing needs of the students in the class.

For the past few years, we have ended up using large index cards containing a student's name on each card, held together by a metal ring. The class librarians are in charge of writing down the books being checked out on the cards and crossing off the names of any books being checked back in. This procedure makes it easy to see the names of the books a child has been reading, and it provides a record of the child's selections during the course of the school year. By year's end, these cards find their way into each child's literacy portfolio.

At the end of each school day, I use these cards to call off each student's name as I dismiss them individually. I ask everyone about the books they will be reading that night. This helps me keep track of each student's reading selections and makes for a more personalized way to say goodbye to each student. It also serves to remind students that they must always take a book home and that they are expected to read something every night.

The classroom library needs to be an inviting place where children enjoy browsing through the collection of reading materials and are able to locate particular resources when they need them. In and around the classroom library, my students' colorful posters adorn the walls, and comfortable places to read are readily available. I want the classroom library to resemble those high-end retail bookstores I mentioned earlier, to be a "palace" for literature, if you will, a place that children just can't stay away from.

Other Shared Experiences

Before leaving this section, I would like to talk about other "shared experiences" that I have used and found successful in developing our learning community. Though I don't believe that building community can be reduced to these planned experiences alone, they help create the opportunity for students to share their lives and listen to the stories of others. This sharing of our beliefs, ideas, and stories becomes the foundation upon which we build our learning community.

Singing

One of the most important community-building experiences we do as a class every day is sing together. I have been playing guitar for over thirty years and have a guitar that remains in the classroom during the school year. Each day we begin by singing a new song for the week and an old favorite. Students hear a new song on Monday, practice it with me on Tuesday and Wednesday, and sing along and play tambourines and other instruments by Thursday and Friday. We discuss what we think the lyrics of the song are about and how the song makes us feel. It is an important daily celebration that students look forward to. We have sung songs by such contemporary artists as Jimmy Buffett, Trisha Yearwood, and Bonnie Raitt, as well as multicultural folk songs from Ireland, Italy, Africa, and Australia.

Food

Along with music, we also share food and our cooking traditions with each other. I love to cook, and even more important, I love to share what I cook. I usually teach my students how to make pasta the way my father taught me, and the way his mother taught him. We mix eggs, salt, and semolina flour together, roll out the dough, cut the fettuccine, and prepare some tomato sauce. Then, of course, we eat. Food plays an important role in the rituals and celebrations we have outside of school, therefore we should include them in our classroom rituals as well.

33

Students bring in various dishes from home that represent their cultures and backgrounds to share with the class. This sharing plays an important role in the building of our community. In the past we have shared potato latkes during Hanukkah, tamales at Christmas, corned beef on St. Patrick's Day, and Vegemite from Australia.

Shoebox Autobiographies

Another important planned experience that I begin the year with is the creation of our "shoebox autobiographies." During the first week of school, I have students take a shoebox and fill it at home with artifacts that they feel symbolize them as individuals. These boxes come to school filled with CDs, photographs, letters, books, toys, cards, and other treasured items. We meet in small groups and share our shoebox autobiographies with each other. These boxes serve as a window into our identities and our cultural backgrounds. By sharing these boxes, we learn about each other, the things we have in common, and the unique interests we bring to our learning community.

"Wallfolios"

Often, these shoebox autobiographies become the impetus for our learning portfolios and the beginnings of our reflections about ourselves as people and as learners. Early in the year, I make available a two-foot-square patch of wall space for students to display the contents of their shoebox autobiographies or things they bring in from home. We call these our "wallfolios." These serve as visual representations of our life histories and experiences. Visitors to our classroom may wander through the room and get to know more about each of us by looking at our wallfolios. This project helps students realize that their individual experiences, cultural backgrounds, and personalities are an important part of our learning community. I always take part in these planned experiences, so that students can get to know me as I get to know them. The more we learn about each other, the more we are able to work together successfully. As a class, we gather our ideas and write about these wallfolios. We put these published pieces in a class book that is available to read during the school year. It becomes a permanent artifact of our learning community.

Class Meeting

Another planned experience that I want to mention is our class meeting, a time when we gather as a class to solve any problems that have arisen during the day. In the beginning of the year, we meet daily, and then approximately twice a week thereafter. Students write down any ideas or challenges they have on our class meeting board. Things like seating arrangements, library procedures, and disagreements with other students are included in these meetings. We gather together in our meeting area and try to solve any problems.

A student is selected as "class meeting director" and serves a one-month term of office. We take nominations and hold an election for this important position. This person then serves as the director of the class meeting discussions, using the ideas written about on the class meeting board to begin the meeting. The class meeting continues until all problems are solved or we run out of time for the day's meeting. By selecting a student to serve as director, I hope to limit my role in these discussions. The more I can step out and allow students to solve their own problems, the more they accept responsibility for the decisions made and the direction of the classroom community. This is a yearlong, if not lifelong, process. We need to learn how to listen to each other, understand each other's needs and interests, and find ways to solve these issues by including everyone's voices in our decisions.

When students come to me with problems that I feel are better handled during the class meeting, I tell them to see the director and put their ideas on our class meeting board for the next meeting. This helps to take care of many of the small issues and keeps me from acting as sole evaluator and solver of my student's problems. Sometimes it's hard to stay out of the discussions, but the more I stay out, the more students assume responsibility for our community and their behavior. An effective learning community is built not only upon students being able to work together effectively, but also on their working independently to solve many of their problems without help from the teacher.

Reflections

I don't want to paint an overly idealistic picture here. The structures that I have described are not in place as the year begins, nor do they simply come into being. These procedures and routines are established over time and are constantly being revised and revisited. As the year unfolds, I introduce new procedures s-l-o-w-l-y, to maintain consistency and predictability during the reading workshop. Children need to understand the routines and the classroom expectations if they are going to assume responsibility for their actions and their learning. Since I expect my students to assume a great deal of responsibility in our classroom, sudden changes in the routines of the workshop can often be unsettling for them.

The learning community and the physical arrangements of the classroom change over the course of the school year as children's needs and interests evolve. The expectations, procedures, and routines that we establish must be responsive to the needs of the community and be easily modified to reflect our growth. The reading workshop is situated among these routines, expectations, and procedures of the learning community. It will have its own set of expectations and routines that evolve as the community comes together.

The physical arrangement of the classroom plays a minor role in the development of a learning environment when compared to the social interactions of the classroom community. As members of our classroom, we create a caring, democratic learning community by sharing our life experiences, negotiating the procedures and rules we live by, sharing favorite stories, discussing our ideas and beliefs, and becoming involved in each others' lives as we learn and grow together.

Community is often defined as a collection of people who see themselves as members of a group that shares common goals and beliefs. The type of community that we build together in our classrooms needs to support the kind of people that we want inhabiting our world outside of schools. In other words, the social interactions in our classrooms serve as models for the types of interactions we want to occur in the outside world. A caring, learning community is a dynamic, ever-changing entity that evolves with the interactions and events that take place during the school year.

Whenever I am struggling with procedures, or the routines we have created aren't running as smoothly as I feel they should, I slow down and think through my set of guiding principles described earlier. Are my practices aligned with my theoretical understandings? Have I provided the learning experiences that are necessary to support learners? Am I trying to introduce too many things, too fast? These are some of the questions I often ask myself.

Trying to do too much at once is a typical problem in making the transition to this type of teaching and classroom structure. You read about classrooms, or visit someone else's classroom, where a literature-based framework is in place, and you want your classroom to run as smoothly as the ones you see and read about. Believe me, it takes a great deal of time and patience for these other teachers to get to the point where things run smoothly and children are responsible for the routines and jobs in the reading workshop.

Slow down! Enjoy your students. Try new things one at a time. When in doubt, read a funny story and laugh with your students. It's always important to remember why you are there: your love for children and your concern for their development.

I have provided you with a diagram of my room arrangement to help you visualize the space I have created in my classroom. Along with this diagram, you will find a list of books that I read during the year to my class that provides an opportunity for the class to discuss issues pertaining to community. These books help us to understand the aspects of living together during the school year. To help you understand my whole day and how the reading workshop is scheduled, I have included my daily schedule and an annotated description for each section of my day.

36

Further Readings

BRIDGES, LOIS. 1996. *Creating Your Classroom Community*. Portland, ME: Stenhouse.

CHAMBERS, AIDAN. 1996. *The Reading Environment: How Adults Help Children Enjoy Books*. Portland, ME: Stenhouse.

PETERSON, RALPH. *Life in a Crowded Place: Making a Learning Community*. Portsmouth, NH: Heinemann.

SHORT, KATHY G., JEROME C. HARSTE, AND CAROLYN BURKE. 1996. *Creating Classrooms for Authors and Inquirers*. Second Edition. Portsmouth, NH: Heinemann.

8:15–8:30	Share Response Logs
8:30–8:45	Community Share/Sing-Along
8:45–10:00	Reading Workshop
10:00–11:00	Writing Workshop
11:00–11:50	Math Workshop
11:50–12:30	Lunch/Recess
12:30–1:00	Poem du Jour/Monopoly/Class Meeting
1:00–2:00	Sciences/Inquiry Workshop
2:00–2:30	Educational Games
2:30–2:45	Reflection Logs
2:45–3:10	Chapter Book Read Aloud
3:10	Dismissal

Figure 3–3. *Daily Schedule*

Share Response Logs: Students gather in pairs to share their homework. Each night they read for half an hour and respond in their lit logs. These logs are described in Chapter 9, "Evaluations."

Community Share/Sing-Along: We begin each day with students sharing special events in their lives with the class. This way we all know what is happening in each others' lives. Then we sing a new song each week as I play guitar, and sing a favorite we learned earlier in the year.

Reading Workshop: This one-hour block of time is the focus of this book!

Writing Workshop: This one-hour block supports students' writing in their writer's notebooks, sharing their writing, editing pieces, and publishing their work. Time is allocated for individual projects and author's chair.

Math Workshop: This hour block is a hands-on workshop, utilizing math manipulatives to help students acquire problem-solving strategies and mathematical thinking. It is set up like a workshop, with minilessons, group work, and a sharing circle.

Poem du Jour/Monopoly/Class Meeting: Each day we read and discuss a new poem. Students sign up to share their favorite poems. We play Monopoly as a class every day. There are two teams, and every day each team gets one roll. The students do the math necessary to keep track of their team and their money. Two days a week we have a class meeting to solve any challenges or offer any new ideas.

Science/Inquiry Workshop: This one-hour block is based on thematic inquiry projects. We study both science and social studies topics such as geology, the Grand Canyon, the water cycle, biology, electricity, and geography. Many of the activities are hands on or research based.

Educational Games: Every day we have a half-hour block when students play educational games like Scrabble, backgammon, chess, checkers, and others I create based on the units of study we have finished.

Reflection Logs: Each day we spend about fifteen to twenty minutes reflecting on our day and writing in our journals. This is described in detail in Chapter 9, "Evaluations."

Chapter Book Read Aloud: I end each day by reading for about half an hour from one of various chapter books. I always read that year's Newbery winner and other pieces of quality literature. There is time for students to discuss the book before we leave for home.

Figure 3–4. *Schedule Expanded*

Lesson Plans **Day:** _____

Opening Ceremonies: newspaper, attendance, lit logs, schedule,
  sharing

Math Challenge:

Reading Workshop

Literary Focus:

Read Aloud:

Minilesson:

Lit Groups: (ok)

Strategy Groups:

Writing Workshop

Unit of Study:

Minilesson:

Teacher Conferences:

Poetry Book of the Week

Song of the Week:

Drama/Art Workshop:

Afternoon Ceremonies: Monopoly, Poem du Jour, Class Meeting

Math Workshop

Science Workshop

Figure 3–5. *Lesson Plan Format*

4

Inside the Reading Workshop: A Typical Focus Unit

*Picture books ... give children the opportunity to engage in an unend-
ing process of meaning making as every rereading brings about new
ways of looking at words and pictures. In other words, picture books
allow children to have multiple experiences as they engage in creating
new meanings and constructing new worlds.*

LAWRENCE SIPE

Let's now examine a "typical" focus unit in order to get a better understanding
of the curricular components that make up my reading workshop. These curricular components operate over time to give the reading workshop direction
and consistency. This chapter describes a typical focus unit to provide you
with the overall picture of what one looks like in my classroom. Each of the
individual curricular components will be explained in detail in the succeeding
chapters.

A focus unit is a series of literary experiences that revolves around a central
theme or focus, such as the works of a particular author, a content topic like
geology, or a theme like freedom or immigration. Over the course of a few weeks,
students read and explore books and other reading materials that focus on
the topic, author, theme, or genre. These focus units are substantially different
from traditional "thematic units" in that they are created with the students, as
we inquire into a particular topic or focus together. These focus units are not sets
of cute activities created over the summer by groups of teachers or commercial
publishing companies; rather, they are a focused inquiry that evolves as student
interact with various texts and resources and build connections to the central
focus.

A Typical Focus Unit: Fictional Narrative

As I described in Chapter 3, I begin each year with a focus unit on "Living Together Differently." This initial focus unit on building community not only helps students understand the concepts of diversity and respect for their fellow classmates, but also gives them the opportunity to become acquainted with the procedures and routines of the reading workshop. Once the reading workshop is running smoothly, it is time to launch another focus unit. For this example, I will describe a unit that focuses on a particular genre. These focus units last for approximately two to five weeks, depending on the level of interest generated, the resources available, and the importance of the particular focus in the overall curriculum.

The genre of original story, or fictional narrative, is traditionally included in the curriculum of the intermediate grades. Many of my students begin the year attempting to draft their own original stories, so a focus on this genre also supports what has been happening in our writing workshop. However, before I can begin any focus unit, I need to decide what the actual focus is going to be. Will it include a particular genre, such as fictional narrative in this case, or will it be the works of one author, say Eve Bunting or Chris Van Allsburg, or possibly a theme or contemporary issue like immigration or homelessness? Depending on our state standards and the curriculum mandates from my school district, I choose a focus that supports both my students' needs and interests, as well as these external directives, whenever possible. More often than not, the things that we are interested in are also included in some way in the curriculum guides I am required to follow. In general, I have found that my students' level of interest goes beyond the minimum expectations found in the state-mandated curriculum standards.

Selecting a Focus

One of my favorite stories in all of children's literature is the fictional narrative *Where the Wild Things Are*, by Maurice Sendak. This story is about a boy named Max who escapes the reality of his life to travel to where the Wild Things live. He ends up being crowned King of the Wild Things, but returns home to find his hot supper waiting for him. This story is one of many in children's literature where the main character is a child who uses his or her imagination to escape from the problems and boredom of his or her life. Because of this prominent theme in children's literature—and in children's lives, for that matter—I decided to create a focus unit around the theme "Escaping Reality."

As a reader of children's picture books, I began to notice the abundance of stories that revolved around the theme of children leaving the reality of their lives by escaping into worlds they created for themselves. Because of this, I gathered together a variety of books that shared this common theme, and used them to create a unit on "Escaping Reality." This unit also served to address the requirement in our curriculum for a genre study on fictional narratives. I usually create five or six major focus units each year, focusing on genres or themes that are included in the Language Arts curriculum, or ones that emerge from the interests of my students or the events that take place in school that year. Along with these major focus units, I also include several smaller units based on children's interests and the experiences we have in the school year. In past years, I have created focus units on fairy tales, postcards, alphabet books, calendars, brochures, and myths and legends, to go along with the more traditional units on nonfiction, letters, poetry, personal narratives, and original stories.

During the unit on Escaping Reality, we read different stories in which the main characters are children who use their imaginations to escape from the problems they are facing or the situations they encounter in their lives. Of course, there are many other connections to these various texts, but this is the primary focus I use in selecting the books to be read during this unit. I have provided a list of the books I have used in the Escaping Reality focus unit (see Figure 4–1).

The book *Where the Wild Things Are* will be used as a "prototypical" example of the fictional narrative genre. Because of this, we will be spending an extensive amount of time reading this story and discussing the various elements of literature used to create this piece of literature. By revisiting this story each day for about a week, I hope that my students will begin to read in a different manner, taking their time to investigate the layers of meanings, the intricate illustrations, and the beautiful language used in this book. Using our experiences with this one particular story, we will make connections to the other stories we will be sharing in this unit and to our own life experiences. *Where the Wild Things Are* will serve as a "cornerstone" book for our focus unit on the genre of fictional narrative and the theme of escaping reality.

Impressions, Connections, and Wonderings

I begin the unit by reading aloud *Where the Wild Things Are* to the whole class. I allow plenty of time to talk about our first impressions of the book, and we share any memories we might have from previous experiences with this popular work of children's literature. Many of my students have read this story before and they often share ideas about what they remember. This first discussion serves as an introduction to the story. Many students make connections to their experiences about being sent to bed without supper, or about dealing with their parents when they are upset.

The next day, I take out the book again and begin to read it for a second time. Some students remind me that we just read this book yesterday and wonder why

BURNINGHAM, JOHN. 1999. *Hey Get Off Our Train*. Topeka: Econo-Clad Books.

COWAN, CATHERINE. 1997. My *Life with the Wave*. Based on the story by Octavio Paz. New York: Lothrop, Lee and Shepard.

HUTCHINS, HAZEL. 1990. *Nicholas at the Library*. Buffalo: Annick Press.

JOYCE, WILLIAM. 2000. *George Shrinks*. New York: HarperCollins Children's Books.

KEATS, EZRA JACK. 1987. *Regards to the Man in the Moon*. New York: Aladdin.

MAZER, ANNE. 1991. *The Salamander Room*. New York: Knopf.

PITTMAN, HELENA CLARE. 1993. *Once When I Was Scared*. New York: Puffin.

RINGGOLD, FAITH. 1996. *Tar Beach*. Albuquerque: Dragonfly.

ROOT, PHYLLIS. 1985. *Moon Tiger*. New York: Henry Holt.

SENDAK, MAURICE. 1988. *Where the Wild Things Are*. New York: HarperCollins Children's Books.

TEAGUE, MARK. 1994. *The Field Beyond the Outfield*. New York: Scholastic.

THOMPSON, COLIN. 1998. *The Paradise Garden*. New York: Knopf.

VAN ALLSBURG, CHRIS. 1990. *Just a Dream*. Boston: Houghton Mifflin Juvenile Books.

Figure 4–1. *Escaping Reality Book List*

we are reading it again. I explain that I would like to read the story a second time, just to see if there are any other connections we can make to the story. Our discussion goes on much longer this time, as children try out new ideas and make new connections to the text and illustrations. Students begin to generate questions and new ideas about the book, so I know that it is time to create a chart for our "Impressions, Connections, and Wonderings."

I have hung a piece of butcher paper behind my reading chair, so I turn and explain the purpose of the chart and the words "Impressions, Connections, and Wonderings," written along the top of the paper (see Figure 4–2). The word *impressions* may be defined as an effect produced on the mind, an uncertain idea or belief; *connections* are ideas that relate to other texts or to experiences of the reader; and *wonderings* refers to the questions and confusions we may encounter during the reading of a text. Some children want to know how Max could come back after traveling "in and out of weeks and through a day" (Sendak, 1961) and

Impressions

Max sailed for a long time.

If I was Max, I would be scared of the Wild Things.

Max was playing and he lost track of time, so he didn't see his mom put the food in his room.

Max's imagination was faster than real time.

Max got bored of the Wild Things and wanted to go home because there were more toys there.

Max frightened the Wild Things.

It was funny when Max said he would eat his mom, and the Wild Things said they would eat Max.

Max fell asleep and imagined what HIS world looked like.

Max is outspoken.

The Wild Things acted like little children, because they said, "I'll eat you up!" just like Max did.

The picture Max drew in the hallway was one of the Wild Things.

Max's wolf suit is a Halloween costume.

When Max wanted to be where someone loved him best of all, it was with his mother.

When Max told the Wild Things to go to bed without their supper, he was acting like his mom.

Connections

Max reminds me of my brother, because he is always getting sent to bed.

This book reminds me of the movie *George of the Jungle*, because he lives in a forest.

In the other book we read, *Higglety, Pigglety Pop*, Sendak had a white dog like Max's.

I imagine things in my closet when I go to bed.

I like to play in my room, and I make my bed a forest sometimes.

I got sent to bed without my supper before, but my mom gave me a snack.

Wonderings

I wonder if Max fell asleep for a couple of minutes and then woke up?

Did Max use his imagination to make the trees grow?

Did Max's mom call him, and then he woke up?

How could Max's food still be hot?

How could Max smell his food from that far away?

Why was Max scared of the Wild Things?

Why did Max wear a wolf suit?

Why did they make Max the King?

How long did he travel?

Did Max get lonely because he sent the Wild Things to bed?

What is a "rumpus"?

Figure 4–2. *Impressions, Connections, and Wonderings Chart*

still have a hot supper. Others think that maybe he was dreaming all of the time and never left the room. They look closely at the illustrations and the text for clues to back up their impressions and connections. Students offer new ideas during our discussions as each child considers what the text means for them in light of the ideas others present.

By the third day, my students are prepared when I take out *Where the Wild Things Are* again and begin to read it for the third time. One boy asks if we will read every book this year three times. I explain that we won't read every book this way, just some of the special cornerstone books that we will use to introduce different focus units. I want them to understand that not only is it permissible to revisit books again and again—and that this type of critical, reflective reading is allowed—but also that it is encouraged, supported, and celebrated in our room. We are trying to act like explorers, uncovering the hidden layers of meaning found in the literature we will share together. In order for students to become explorers themselves, I must demonstrate this type of reading and thinking, and model my own comprehension processes as I read the book to them.

I want my students to understand that reading is "making sense," coming to deeper connections between a text and our experiences, and that we can't always make sense of a story the first time we read through it. I want them to feel free to go back and reread a story to "dig deeper," to explore the layers of meaning inherent in a quality piece of literature. I know that this type of critical reflection concerning our reading, and these lengthy discussions of a single piece of literature, will help support the "passionate attention" students will need to be successful in our literature study groups later in the year. I also know that this type of reading may not have been supported in some of the other classrooms my students have been in during their previous years of schooling. This critical, reflective stance toward reading and literature may be new to many children in my class. I need to be patient and understanding in order to support my students' development as critical readers and explorers of literature.

After reading the story for the third time, I take out a set of multiple copies of *Where the Wild Things Are* so children can read and revisit the book on their own or in small groups. Providing time for students to explore books independently and in small groups allows children the opportunity to reconsider ideas about their readings in light of the discussions we have already had, share new ideas with their friends, closely examine the text and the illustrations, and reread the book at their own pace. After an extended period of time reading and discussing the book, students return to the group with more ideas for our discussion, and they offer new thoughts and insights that we can include in our "Impressions, Connections, and Wonderings" chart.

As this chart begins to fill with ideas, I turn to a new chart that I will use and refer to often during this focus unit. This new chart is called a "comparison chart" (see Figure 4–3). I use this chart to create a visual representation of the books we are reading and the elements of literature that I want to call students' attention to. This chart helps children make connections across titles as well as within a particular story.

In the left-hand column of the chart, I list the titles of the books that we have read; along the top row of the chart, I write the elements of literature that I want students to attend to and discuss, such as setting, plot, character, mood, tension, symbols, and point of view. It is my job to recognize these elements when they come up in our discussions, and draw students' attention to how the author uses them in the stories we are reading. For example, after reading *Where the Wild Things Are*, students offer ideas about the character Max, the setting of the story, the tension concerning whether Max will return home, and the hot supper as a symbol of unconditional love.

As our unit continues, students bring up various elements of literature in their small-group and whole-class discussions. They may not refer to these elements by name, saying, "the setting of the story is . . . ," but they know from their previous experiences with stories that each story takes place somewhere, at some particular time, and contains characters who act in the story. As students talk about these elements, I begin to introduce the language of the elements of literature into our discussions, saying, for example, that the place and the time a story is set is called the setting. In this way, I am helping students learn the "language of literature" and I am calling conscious attention to particular elements of the story, rather than giving out standard dictionary definitions for these elements of literature. Not only do I want students to be able to recognize these various elements, I also want them to understand how they affect the overall story and how authors use them to construct their unique fictional narratives. For this particular focus unit, I want students to begin to understand how Maurice Sendak used the setting, tension, and characters to weave together such an impressive and intricate story.

The next day when students enter the room, they notice that I have taken apart two old paperback copies of *Where the Wild Things Are* and displayed the illustrations along one wall of the room in storyboard fashion. By displaying the pages of the book in this manner, we are able to see all of the illustrations at once and bring a new perspective to our discussions. Suddenly, my students are talking about how the pictures get larger as the story progresses until they became three double-page spreads with no text at all. They notice that these double-page illustrations coincide with the part of the story where Max declares, "Let the wild rumpus start!" The students also notice that after this part of the story, the pictures get smaller until the last page, where Sendak has included no illustrations and

Title	Characters	Setting	Mood	Point of View
Where the Wild Things Are	Max: big imagination, rude, bossy, hungry, bored, changes mood, mischievous, acts like his mother, wolf suit, feels sorry for mom at end of story	House, room changes into a forest, sailed to Wild Things, closet, blanket, past tense	Max gets angry, room changes, sad, he goes back, Mom is frustrated, Wild Things are caring	Narrator, how Max sees the world
Humphrey's Bear	Humphrey: boy, cares about his bear, sleeps with bear, dreams, adventures, it's his dad's bear, brave	Humphrey's room, backyard, river, sea, island, dreams, imagination, windows, present tense	Dad is sad about telling him he is too old for a bear, happy ending, brave, not scared	Narrator, third person
The Salamander Room	Brian: young boy, imagination, likes animals, persistent, responsible, has a plan	Expanding room, imagination, makes his own home, future tense	Happy, hopeful, excited, relieved at end	Brian's perspective, 1st person
Moon Tiger	Jessica Ellen: girl, not scared of tigers, has a brother, jealous, thinks bro is annoying	Bedroom, out the window, parents downstairs, forest, with the tiger	Jealous, sibling rivalry, nice to the tiger, angry	Jessica's perspective, 1st person future tense
The Paradise Garden	Peter: boy, doesn't like noise, stressed, plans his escape, deep emotions about family, looking for peace	City=noise, packed, busy, stressful, drab. Garden= peace, quiet, big, beautiful, silent colorful, calm, slow	Lonely, happy in the garden, sad about his family	Peter's perspective, narrator, 3rd person

Figure 4–3. *Comparison Chart 1*

simply writes, "and it was still hot." During the ensuing discussions, students offer impressions, connections, and wonderings that probably would never have occurred to them if I hadn't taken apart the book and displayed it in this manner. By altering the way we see the text, I have been able to provide a new perspective for students to make meanings as they transact with the text and the illustrations.

When we begin the reading workshop the next day, I have taken the words from the book and typed them up on a single sheet of paper. I keep the same format in which the words appear in the original text, using the same line breaks and paragraph structure, but this time I have not included any of the illustrations for our discussion Students remark that the words in the book now look like a poem, and that some of the words are in capital letters. By "disrupting" the text once again, focusing this time on the text separate from the illustrations, I offer students yet another perspective from which to consider this book. These disruptions allow us to offer new impressions, connections, and wonderings that we will include on our chart.

Multiple copies of the book have been available for students to read and revisit since we began discussing this book. I have begun to notice that students are talking about the book and sharing ideas with each other during different parts of our day. Our charts are filling up with ideas, we are exploring many new interpretations, and we have made personal and literary connections to Max and the Wild Things during the week. I believe that it's time to introduce a new story.

Relating to Other Books

The following Monday, I begin the reading workshop by choosing a new book from the list of books I have available for this focus unit. This one is called *Humphrey's Bear*, by Jan Wahl, illustrated by William Joyce. In this story, a father questions his son's attachment to his teddy bear, and wonders if his son isn't too old for that kind of toy. At night, the bear grows larger and takes Humphrey on an adventure, through his bedroom window and out to sea. When Humphrey returns to his room, he drops the bear from his bed and cries out for it. His father hears his cries, and as Humphrey wakes up, his father hands the bear to him as he recalls his own adventures with the same bear when he was a child.

It doesn't take long for students to make connections between the characters of Max and Humphrey, the adventures out to sea, and the return to reality in these two books. Because we spent an extensive amount of time with the first book, in this case *Where the Wild Things Are*, children understand that I expect them to read more critically, digging into the layers of meaning and the experiences we bring to each new story. Each day for the next few weeks, we read and discuss a new book. As we read each book from our list of stories, the discussions take us in new directions and help us to build new connections to the theme of escaping reality.

As each new book in the unit is read, it is placed in a special book rack so that children can revisit them whenever they wish. This book rack is surrounded by the charts we have been creating that contain our impressions, connections, and wonderings about the various pieces of literature in this particular focus unit. When someone enters our room, they will easily see what we have been reading and studying. The charts and diagrams we have created so far help us to make connections over time, represent our "trail" of thoughts, and allow others to see where we have been in our discussions. After the unit is over, these books will be shelved in a special box that will be labeled "Escaping Reality Books" and decorated by my students. Each ensuing focus unit will have its own box when we are finished.

Returning to the comparison chart that focuses on the different stories we have read in this unit, we begin to notice some patterns and relationships among the various books and add these new categories to the comparison chart. This focus unit, for example, includes the symbol of the moon, the relationships between the main character and their parents, imagination, food as a symbol of unconditional love, the concept of growing up, and the idea of traveling in our sleep or dreams (see Figure 4–4). These categories are not as generic as the categories included in the first example of the comparison chart, and are more specific to the books we are reading in this particular focus unit. What were rather simple comments regarding the elements of literature at the beginning of this study are now complex connections to the various categories and relationships in the specific texts we have experienced. This second comparison chart has helped us to move beyond labeling the various elements of literature, to being able to discuss how these elements affect the story and how the author uses them to enhance the story.

Although I had tentatively chosen the books I planned to read in this unit before the study began, I added other titles and changed the order I read the books to fit our discussions. For example, at one point in the study, the children seemed to be focusing on the idea of things "growing" in the books. For the next read aloud, I chose a book where nothing grew. This extended the discussions in a new direction. In this instance, I was not trying to direct the discussion; rather, I was trying to provide experiences that would help children explore new interpretations and other possible connections.

We ended up reading about ten books in this particular focus unit. We charted our ideas, discussed each new story, and developed more complex relationships between the stories we read together. We were able to adopt a new, more reflective stance to our readings because of the close, passionate attention we gave to these books, especially *Where the Wild Things Are*. We became explorers of the meanings in these various pieces of literature.

Title	Things Grow	Imagination	Time of Day	Setting	Going to Bed	Problem	Ending
Where the Wild Things Are	Forest grew in Max's bedroom	Max imagined the forest, water, and wild things	Started at night, went through a day, back to night	House, his room, forest where wild things are	Sent to his room with no supper	Sent to his room because he was bad	Max came back, food was hot, WTs disappear
Humphrey's Bear	The bear grew	Humph had a good imagination	Nighttime dreaming	Bedroom, ocean	Went to bed with his bear	Dad didn't want H. to have his bear	H. came home with the bear
George Shrinks	George thought things grew, but he shrank	George imagined he was small to go on adventure	Day or early morning	George's house, bed, outside	Woke up in bed	George shrank	Parents came home, G. woke up in bed
Moon Tiger	Nothing	Real tiger came in the room	Nighttime	Girl's room, North Pole, forest	Sent to bed for not helping brother	She didn't listen to her mom	Jessica falls asleep. She imagined it

Figure 4–4. *Comparison Chart 2*

Extending Our Understandings

I usually close out the focus unit with some sort of drama, art, or music experience that extends the connections and ideas we have been exploring. For this unit, in this particular year, I asked the children to go back and reread *Where the Wild Things Are* and think about other ways we could tell or present this story. I asked the students to try and think of other forms of expression, such as poetry, brochures, invitations, photography, art, music, and drama, that could be used to tell the story of Max and the Wild Things. This type of writing is often referred to as "multigenre" writing, and my students ended up writing in many of these genres, or forms of expression. They created brochures, maps, rap songs, skits, poems, and letters to Max, and they conducted an imaginary interview with several of the characters. The only things that limited this experience were the students' imagination and our classroom's art supplies.

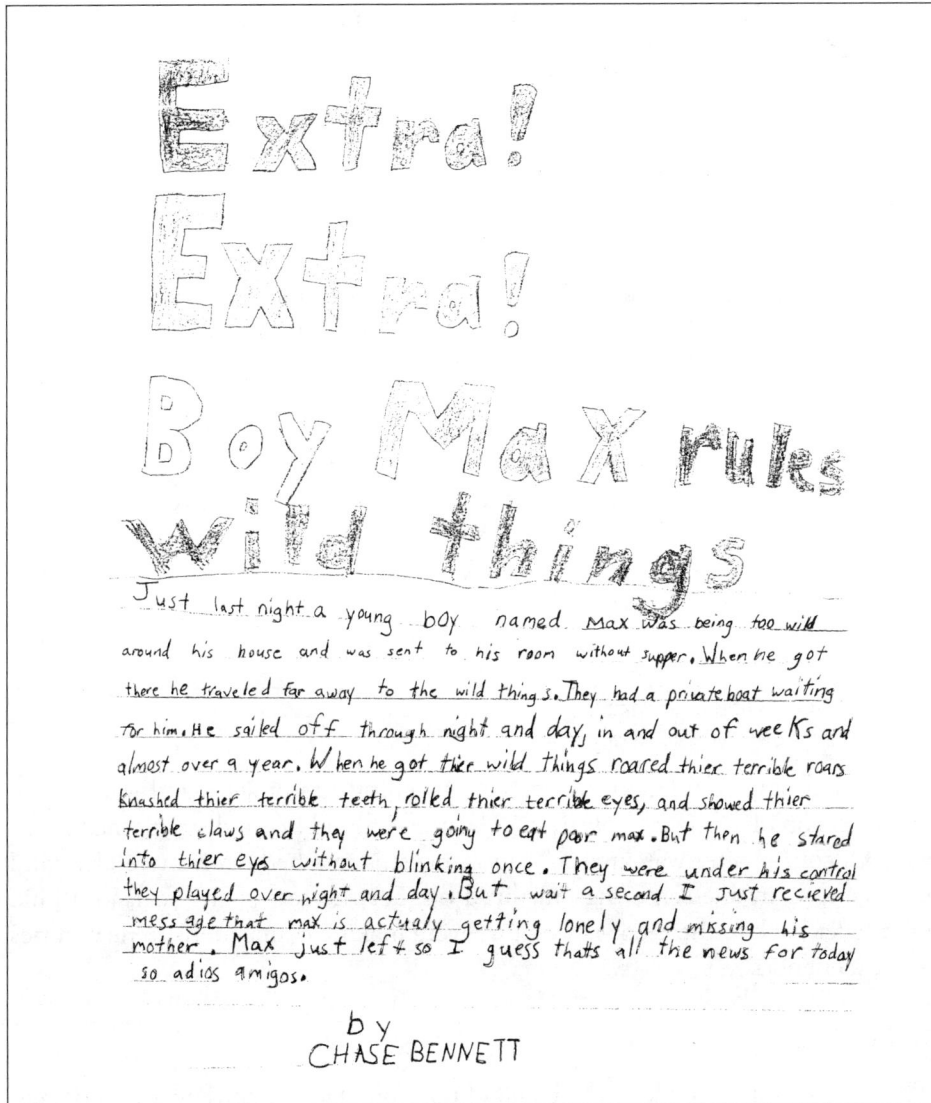

Just last night a young boy named Max was being too wild around his house and was sent to his room without supper. When he got there he traveled far away to the wild things. They had a private boat waiting for him. He sailed off through night and day, in and out of weeks and almost over a year. When he got thier wild things roared thier terrible roars knashed thier terrible teeth, rolled thier terrible eyes, and showed thier terrible claws and they were going to eat poor max. But then he stared into thier eyes without blinking once. They were under his control they played over night and day. But wait a second I just recieved message that max is actualy getting lonely and missing his mother. Max just left so I guess thats all the news for today so adios amigos.

by
CHASE BENNETT

Figure 4–5a. *Multigenre Example*

Missing "Have you seen him ?"

Name: Max
Age: 8 and 3months
Time missing: just before dinner time.
Last wearing: white wolf suit.
Last seen: sailing in a red boat.
The place he was going: Where the
Wild Things are.

Mother's statement:
"I just sent him to
his room, for chasing
the dog with a fork,
and running around
like a Wild Thing.
My dear sweet little
guy."

Wild Things Statement:
"We didn't want him
to go. We told him we
would eat him up, but
we didn't mean it. We
just didn't want him
to go."

Please, contact us at 1-800-missing.
Thank you, We hope to be hearing from you
as soon as possible.

We are in a search to find Max. We will
with your help. So please, call.

Figure 4–5b. *Multigenre Example*

As a closing celebration, we shared our multigenre projects and watched an opera version of *Where the Wild Things Are* that I found in our district's media catalog. Of course, after watching the video, my students had many more ideas and questions, so in one sense the unit lived on. For the rest of the year, we would often refer back to these books when we were making connections to new stories and experiences.

Reflections

This unit was an example of the blend of both preplanned curricular experiences and response-centered instruction that occurs in all of my focus units. Some of the

Alan's Character Interview

ALAN: Welcome to Character Interview. Today we will be welcoming Max from *Where the Wild Things Are*. His story is being too imaginative. Oh, let's bring out our guest.

MAX: Hi everybody.

ALAN: Welcome to the show Max. My first question is where did you get that wild wolf suit?

MAX: Well, I got it at a costume shop for Halloween and every time I wore it my imagination shot up.

ALAN: Really? Anyways, my second question is how did your mom feel when you told her I'll eat you up?

MAX: Umm. . . . No comment.

ALAN: O.K. My next question is how did you make that forest grow in your room?

MAX: Well Alan, it's all about imagination.

ALAN: Oh.

MAX: Hmm. . . . Alan what time is it?

ALAN: Well, it's almost 7:30.

MAX: Uh-oh, I'm gonna miss dinner! Bye.

ALAN: Wait, I still have more questions.

MAX: Sorry

ALAN: But I, I, uhh

ALAN: Since our guest left we have to end the show.

Figure 4–5c. *Multigenre Example*

experiences I planned before we started, and some of the things, like the multi-genre study, came to me during the course of the unit. I feel that this flexibility in my lesson planning is crucial to being able to respond to the needs and interests of my students. Although I had in mind some ideas about where the discussions might lead us and what books I intended to read to my students, I was always mindful of their perspectives, ready and willing to rethink the experiences I would provide, in order to respond to new insights.

I hope this second look inside the reading workshop helps you to see how it operates over time. Now that you have followed one particular focus unit, I expect you have a better understanding of how to develop one of these units for your own classroom. For me this is the hardest part of teaching: having a vision for where you are headed, while still providing the necessary foundation for students to make sense of new experiences. It is the blend of planning ahead and responding to the experiences and ideas that arise that makes teaching in a literature-based classroom successful.

5

Invitations: Bringing Children and Literature Together

You can't make people read. Any more that you can
make them love, or dream.

DANIEL PENNAC

Ralph Peterson, an author and professor at Arizona State University, once told me that you can't force people into reading or sharing their ideas. And although I always believed him, it took me several years to understand how deeply this statement affected my beliefs about reading and helping children develop as readers. No matter how much we as teachers would like to believe that we can make children read or directly "teach" children to read, the best we can do is create an environment that supports children's development as readers, work with children to facilitate their understandings and attempts at making meaning from text, and invite them into the world of reading and literature. As the opening quote implies, though we can't *make* children read, through demonstrations and invitations we can *show* children how and why we read, and what awaits them in the world of reading and literature.

By inviting students into the world of literature and creating a space where children have time to read and access to books, we are creating a foundation for our "community of readers" to live within. Shirley Brice Heath once wrote, "children become literate by establishing a bonded relationship with a joyfully literate adult" (1983). As that "joyfully literate adult" in my classroom, I am the "literacy catalyst," the promoter of reading and literature, the ringleader for our community of readers, inviting all my children to become members of our "Literacy Club." We learn to act as readers and as members of our literacy club as much as we learn how to read.

I believe that reading aloud:

1. builds a rich background in literary knowledge and language
2. promotes the joy of reading
3. invites children to experience new and favorite stories
4. helps build a community of readers
5. anchors the sounds of language in children
6. exposes children to new titles, authors, genres, and illustrators
7. provides an opportunity to discuss literature
8. helps children develop their imagination
9. helps children learn how to listen to stories
10. provides a pleasurable community experience

Figure 5–1. *Benefits of Reading Aloud*

Reading Aloud with Children

There are different ways to invite children into the world of literature, but I believe that the best way to begin is by reading books aloud with children every day and inviting them to share their ideas about these books. Along with being an enjoyable activity that develops a sense of community in our classrooms, reading aloud exposes children to a wide variety of authors, stories, genres, and illustrators (see Figure 5–1). It immerses children in daily literary experiences, exposes them to the rich language of quality literature, allows children the opportunity to connect to a wide range of stories, builds the foundation upon which the reading workshop is structured, and demonstrates the kind of "literary explorations" that I will extend in our literature study groups.

People are never too old to be read to. I read aloud with my students every day in classrooms from kindergarten to the graduate-level courses I teach at various universities. Too often, by the intermediate grades, once children have learned to read independently, they are sometimes "abandoned" to their books to read by themselves. What a shame. Reading aloud continues to stimulate the excitement of reading and literature long after children are able to read for themselves. I believe that one of the most influential activities in my intermediate-grade classrooms, as well as my children's literature courses at the college level, is the introduction of new books and authors through reading aloud.

For these reasons, reading aloud is the primary experience I provide for bringing children and literature together and inviting children into the world of reading. You may have noticed that I mainly use the word *with* rather than *to* children when referring to reading aloud. I prefer *with* because I believe that as teachers, we need to be an active part of the read aloud experience. I am not reading "at" children; rather, we are sharing a book together. We talk about the book while we are sharing it, and we discuss our reactions to the text. I offer my ideas, as well as listen carefully to my students' ideas. It is a shared experience, not simply an oral rendition of a text.

Strategies for Reading Aloud

Rather than duplicate a list of read aloud strategies from other excellent resources, such as Jim Trelease's *The New Read-Aloud Handbook*, I will share with you a list of ideas developed by one of my intermediate-grade classes. The students in my class paired up with the children in a kindergarten class once a week for "Reading Buddies," when we got together and shared stories. My students would select a book to read with their kindergarten buddies, and the kindergartners would select a book to read with my students. After trying to read aloud with the kindergartners a few times, my students came up with a list of "Tips for a Successful Reading Buddy Experience" (see Figure 5–2).

Reviewing this list of ideas, it seems to me that making good selections for books to read aloud, reading with enthusiasm, not asking too many questions, and letting children talk about the books are the most important points to remember. When I sit down to read a book to children, there are several things I try to consider. If it is a picture book, I have to decide if I will hold the book so children

1. Hold the book so children can see it.
2. Read with enthusiasm.
3. Read slowly and clearly.
4. Read loud enough so everyone can hear.
5. Let children read along if they want to.
6. Always let children talk about a book if they want to.
7. Let them predict what will happen.
8. Only read books you really like yourself.
9. Pick out books you can read well.
10. Use different voices for different characters.

Figure 5–2. *Tips for a Successful Reading Buddy Experience*

can see the pictures as I read, or wait until the end of each page to share the illustrations. This decision depends upon the book being read, the age of the listeners, and their experience with being read to. It also depends on the book that I am reading. With some books, such as *Just Another Ordinary Day*, by Rod Clement, it is better to read aloud each page first, and then show the students the pictures because of the ironic twists between text and pictures. Other read alouds, wordless picture books, for example, must be shared as you read. Other books can be read while students see the illustrations, especially with younger readers. Big books, for example, are designed so that students can see the illustrations as you are reading the text.

When reading aloud, I have to be sure that I provide ample time for students to view the illustrations. They seem to pay more attention to the illustrations than we adults do. Young readers rely on the illustrations to make sense of the story and need to be able to revisit the pictures as they discuss the book. Because of this, I have a space on the floor where we always sit to read together that is close enough for everyone to see the illustrations, but big enough for everyone to fit comfortably. It is our little "theater in the round." I have a special rocking chair that I sit in when I read, which doubles as the "special guest" chair and the "author's chair" in our writing workshop.

At the end of each school day, I read aloud from a chapter book. During this time, I invite students to get comfortable as I read. They usually end up lying on the floor or on pillows around me to listen as I read. However, this is a "lay around, not play around" time. I set clear expectations that students will remain attentive and listen to the story during this time. I believe that this is our responsibility to expect and reinforce the routines that the students and I have established. It is important for students to understand that they are responsible for actively listening to the story being read. When I explicitly explain and go over my expectations, children learn how to listen and respond to our read aloud events. Besides, if the books that we choose are of high quality, children can't wait to hear the stories. See Figure 5–3 for a list of my favorite read aloud authors.

One final thought about reading aloud. Instead of always reading books aloud with my class myself, I often invite special guests to come and visit our classroom and read with my children. Sharing their favorite stories and books, these special guests demonstrate that people outside of schools love to read, and that it's not just their teacher who has a passion for reading. I have invited principals, superintendents, parents, local celebrities, college students, and my family members to read to my children. My students always seem to look forward to these visits from our special guests, and I try to plan as many as possible during the course of the year.

Dr. Seuss	Jon Sciezska	Rod Clement
Robert Munsch	David Macaulay	Mercer Mayer
William Joyce	Jean Craighead	Chris Van Allsburg
Cynthia Rylant	George	John Burningham
Jane Yolen	Graeme Base	David Weisner
Eve Bunting	Lois Lowry	Madeline L'Engle
Audrey and Don	Jerry Spinelli	Patricia MacLachlan
Wood	Peter Sis	Roald Dahl
Kevin Henkes	Natalie Babbitt	Avi
Helen Lester	Katherine Paterson	Scott O'Dell
Colin Thompson	Mildred Taylor	Anthony Browne
Ann Turner	William Steig	
Babette Cole	Byrd Baylor	
Lane Smith	Mem Fox	

Figure 5–3. *Favorite Read Aloud Authors*

Why Picture Books?

Picture books are works of literature that combine illustrations and text to tell a story and provide information to the reader. The text and the illustrations blend together interdependently to support each other. An important distinction between picture books and other combinations of text and pictures is that with picture books, neither the text nor the illustrations could stand alone and tell the whole story.

Some of the reasons I choose to read picture books on a daily basis are because they are 1) inviting and enjoyable, 2) accessible, 3) replete with beautiful illustrations, 4) complex, and 5) models of a wide variety of structures, genres, topics, or themes. Picture books are concise, highly interactive pieces of literature. Students need to not only listen to the story, but must also interact with the pictures to make sense of the story. Picture books allow children to linger over pictures, revisiting them again and again in their attempts to make meaning with this genre of literature.

Picture books contain wonderful stories that invite children to read and enjoy them. Humorous stories like *A Day with Wilbur Robinson*, by William Joyce, or *The Stinky Cheese Man and Other Fairly Stupid Tales*, by Jon Sciezska, are read again and again by the students in my classroom. Picture books also contain characters and contemporary themes and issues that relate to the lives, backgrounds, and experiences of my students. They are able to relate to the characters and issues in these texts, and are better able to understand the experiences they go through in their own lives.

The quality of the illustrations in contemporary picture books is outstanding. Due to advances in technology, computer graphics, and the printing process, illustrations are more complex and engaging than ever before. I believe that it is the quality of the illustrations and the images contained in these books that draws my students and many adults alike to these pieces of literature.

The stories in children's picture books are easily accessible to young readers. Students can relate to the main characters and the challenges they face in many of these stories. Although these books are not simplistic, the language used in them is generally easy to read, and authors provide supports, such as repetitive texts or patterns, to help young readers make sense of the story. However, young children are not the only ones who enjoy this genre. My intermediate-grade students, as well as my college students and I, love to read and be read to from picture books.

Another reason I choose picture books is the wide variety of themes and topics that can be shared through this medium. The topics range from homelessness in Eve Bunting's *Fly Away Home* to slavery in Ann Turner's *Nettie's Trip South*. With help from librarians, colleagues, booklists, and professional resources, teachers are able to find picture books to fit almost any topic or theme being studied.

One final reason I use picture books so much in my classroom is because I love to read them myself. I genuinely enjoy the illustrations and the stories contained in these books. I often spend many hours, and far too much money, at my favorite bookstore looking through the picture books and adding new titles to my already extensive collection. These books are not just for kids. The stories and illustrations are increasingly complex and offer challenges and new possibilities to both novice and mature readers alike.

I once heard Patricia McKissack read aloud her wonderful story *Flossie and the Fox* at an International Reading Association conference. After hearing her rendition of the story, I went right down to one of the children's literature booksellers and bought the book that very afternoon. I have since been trying to come close to the rich southern dialect that she used to read the book. For me it was an outstanding performance of a great story, and has become a permanent favorite in my read aloud repertoire. Although I don't believe I will ever be able to come close to the way she read the book that day, I will never forget the power of that story and the power of her voice to invite me in.

Access, Time, and Choices

As classroom teachers, we need to provide children with access to a wide variety of reading materials, an extensive, uninterrupted amount of time to read every day, and choices about what is read to them and what they are reading themselves. Children need to know that they will have time to read during the day and that this is something that will not be taken away. In other words, it is not a privilege to be able to read in class, it is every child's right. This time must be given to *all* readers.

We also have to provide a considerable amount of time for children to browse through our library collections to make appropriate choices for their reading. Earlier, I described my trips to the local bookstore near my home, and how much time I gave myself for browsing through the store when I went. The same considerations should be given to children when they are browsing through our libraries. Browsing is not wasting time, it is taking one's time to make an appropriate selection. Although I don't want children wasting time just staring at the library collection, I want to provide them enough time to find the right book for them. By browsing through the classroom and school library collections, children learn more about what is available and what suits their needs and interests.

The largest portion of time in the reading workshop is devoted to exploring books and reading. Whether this time is spent independently, in pairs, or in small groups reading a particular book together, the workshop provides time to read and access to literature. Providing extensive amounts of time for students to read also exposes children to new books, authors, and genres. In my reading workshop, I devote between thirty and fifty minutes for children to interact with texts. Children read independently, in pairs, or in small groups. They read different books of their own choosing, or read one book along with other students. During the beginning of the year, we spend many days discussing how to choose a book and how to find an appropriate place to sit and read for this block of time.

Many children are not used to assuming responsibility for their actions, so we proceed slowly. I want children to be able to sustain their reading for this block of time so that I will be free to work with lit study groups, reading strategy groups, or individual readers. In order to do this there are several things I have to help children be able to do on their own (see Figure 5–4).

These may sound like very simple things that children should be able to do without being taught, but to assume they understand these things is a mistake. I spend considerable time getting these procedures in place so we can get on with our lives in the reading workshop. It takes time, but it is well worth the effort.

The school librarian and the librarian at the local public library have become my strongest allies in helping to bring children and literature together. Each year,

Students are responsible for:

1. choosing their own books and checking them out from the classroom library
2. keeping the library organized
3. finding a place to sit while reading
4. writing in their reading response logs
5. responding to each others' ideas
6. sharing ideas with classmates
7. noticing when their conversation is getting too loud
8. caring for books
9. solving their own problems during the workshop time
10. working together in groups and resolving any conflicts

Figure 5–4. *Student Responsibilities in the Reading Workshop*

the first field trip I try to schedule is to the public library to be sure each child has a library card. These cards provide free access to books and information; many libraries offer summer reading programs, special events, and book sales each year to help support children's development as readers. I hope that these trips to the public library become a ritual in the lives of my students and their families.

Book club orders, book fairs, young authors' days, Read Across America Day, and other special reading events help expose children to the world of literature and focus their attention on the importance of reading. By typing up the lyrics to the songs we sing every day, we transform the sing-along into a shared reading experience. Shared reading is described as a reading approach in which children can follow along with a text, with oral support provided by a fluent reader. Children sing along with me and my guitar, and follow along with the lyrics provided. This is an enjoyable experience that also helps children learn to read.

As I mentioned in my discussion about reading aloud tips, I pair up with another class each school year for "reading buddies." My students match up with younger students in either a kindergarten or first-grade classroom and share stories with them at least once a week. My students feel a sense of pride at being able to share stories with their reading buddies. They choose books that they are able to read well, and they find this a rewarding and successful experience. We usually have an end-of-the-year reading celebration with our buddies to celebrate our time together.

All of the experiences I have just described provide access to literature, time for students to read, and choices about what they read. These three ideas help to invite children into the world of literature and empower them as readers. As classroom teachers, we need to provide invitations that bring children and literature together to help them develop as lifelong readers and assume an active role in their reading.

Selecting Literature

Choosing among the thousands of books published each year can be a daunting task, even for teachers who are experienced with literature-based reading frameworks. The one thing that seems to be true of all teachers I have worked with is that there is never enough money for books. Whether teachers receive monies from their districts for their classroom literature selections or not, I have never heard a teacher say, "Well, I just don't need any more good books in my room this year." As classroom teachers, we often spend large amounts of our own money on reading materials for our classroom because we know the value of having a wide selection of quality reading materials available for our students.

Because of the limited amounts of monies available for literature, we have become more selective with the money we spend on books. The Caldecott and Newbery Award–winning books, and the associated "honors" selections, are two good places to start building a literature collection. Some of my favorite authors and illustrators are included in these lists of award-winning books. These books represent the highest quality of children's literature recognized by librarians and other literary critics. Other books written and illustrated by these same authors and illustrators are good choices for a classroom collection.

There are other awards given to children's literature, like the Coretta Scott King Award for outstanding African American literature, *Reading Rainbow* selections, the *New York Times* Children's Book Award, and the American Library Association book awards. Along with these literature awards, there are numerous booklists that can also be used as a starting point for choosing quality literature, such as the Children's Choices booklist, published in *The Reading Teacher*, the journal of the International Reading Association (IRA), or the book reviews published in *Language Arts*, the journal of the National Council Teachers of English (NCTE). There are literally hundreds of these different booklists available to help teachers make appropriate selections of quality reading materials for their classrooms.

I would have to admit, however, that the strongest influence on the choices I make for my classroom comes from my students themselves. If the books I choose don't make a strong connection to my students, whether they are award-winning

1. use teacher's favorites from previous years
2. return to familiar favorites, the "classics"
3. read other titles from our favorite authors and illustrators
4. use book review suggestions in newspapers and magazines
5. rely on word of mouth—suggestions of teachers, friends, and family
6. browse the school and local library
7. review the Newbery and Caldecott awards
8. ask clerks in the local bookstore
9. read book jackets and advertisements

Figure 5–5. *Criteria for Choosing Books to Read*

books or not, they won't help invite children into the world of literature. With this in mind, I want to share a list from my classroom that we developed to help us choose reading materials for our outside reading and for our classroom collection (see Figure 5–5).

I listen carefully to the choices my students make, the opinions they share about the books we read, and the titles and authors of their favorite books. If the children don't want to hear certain books or read them by themselves, they may not be books worth having in the classroom—at least, not with this particular group. Preferences change from year to year, and no two groups are ever alike. What becomes a favorite with one group is sometimes overlooked by another. However, if children don't like a particular title, and can give reasons for why they don't, I usually decide to read another book. There are just too many excellent books available today to read anything but books children and teachers both enjoy.

As with all rules, there is an exception, of course. I fully believe in and promote the idea that it is not only my job to provide access to the books and reading materials that children want to read, but also to introduce them to books they don't know they want. There's a vast world of literature available to us as readers, and we don't always know what's available or what we might enjoy. To teachers falls the job of introducing children to new books and expanding the collections available to them.

I want to have books available in my classroom that children will revisit again and again. The quality of the writing and the illustrations, along with the appropriateness of the theme and topic, are important considerations as well. I also believe that the topic or the characters in the story should have relevance, meaning, and a strong relationship to the lives of the children in our classrooms. I try to choose books that are thought provoking, moving, powerful, and rich in possibilities. It is this richness that leads to connections and opens up the opportunity for "invested" discussions.

I don't want children choosing books that are too hard for them, because this may frustrate inexperienced readers. However, if children are reading for meaning, they generally do not select books that are too hard for them. As teachers, we should be careful about limiting children's reading selections to only those things we believe they can read independently. Children need time to explore many different books, and if we teach them that reading must first and foremost make sense, and they really understand this concept, then they will make appropriate choices about what they are reading for themselves. Active, lifelong readers choose books for themselves in the same way writers choose their topics to write about. It is under rare circumstances that I ever assign a particular book to my elementary students.

Multicultural Considerations

When selecting books for our classroom library and to read aloud, we need to be sure that we balance traditional titles with books that present nonmainstream topics and perspectives. As the students in our classrooms come from more diverse backgrounds, cultures, locations, and ethnic origins, the books we read should include these diverse perspectives. This does not mean that only literature with diverse perspectives should be used in "inner city" classrooms with children of color, it means that *all* children need to experience multicultural literature and issues in order to be the kind of citizens that support and thrive in a democratic society.

Every book we select reflects a perspective. Whether it is cultural, related to social class, or historical, literature represents a specific set of values and beliefs. As teachers, we need to become aware of our own perspectives concerning our selection of reading materials in our classrooms and in our lives. We need to guard against selecting only those books that seem "natural" or familiar to us, especially as members of the predominantly white, middle-class teaching profession. The values we hold and the perspectives we carry affect the selections we make and the literature we read in our classrooms, and therefore affect the relationships and connections that our students make with the characters and stories they experience. By bringing our potential biases to a conscious level, and by closely scrutinizing the criteria for the literature selections we make, we may be better able to address the issues that challenge us and present a more comprehensive worldview through the literature we select.

The books we choose should:

1. achieve a high degree of cultural accuracy
2. be rich in cultural details
3. contain authentic dialogue
4. contain authentic relationships
5. include in-depth treatment of cultural issues
6. include members of minority populations for a purpose, not merely a quota

Figure 5–6. *Criteria for Selecting Multicultural Literature*

Junko Yukoto (1993) suggested criteria for selecting multicultural literature in an article in *Language Arts*, the journal of the National Council Teachers of English (see Figure 5–6). At the World Congress in Auckland, New Zealand, Jerry Harste and Chris Leland (2000) presented criteria for selecting literature to promote social justice and critical issues (see Figure 5–7). The considerations included in these lists are important if we are to include the lives and backgrounds of all the children who come to our classrooms. We want our classrooms to reflect the kind of world we want to inhabit, and literature can be a powerful voice in this social change.

By addressing the criteria provided above and the suggestions that I have made here, I hope that teachers will expand their read aloud selections, taking into account the cultural, social, and historical diversity of their classrooms and the world in which we live. We need to be sure that all voices are heard and that all viewpoints are accepted in our community of readers.

The literature we select should:

1. make differences among people visible
2. enrich our understanding of history and life by giving voice to those who have been traditionally marginalized in our society
3. show people how to begin to take action concerning social issues
4. help us question why certain groups are positioned as "others"

Figure 5–7. *Criteria for Selecting Literature to Promote Critical Issues*

Reflections

Through the experiences and invitations provided during the reading workshop and throughout our school day, I hope that children find their own doorway into the world of reading and literature. Providing these invitations does not guarantee that all children will cross over, however. If we don't take the time to offer these experiences, to provide these invitations, fewer and fewer of our students will find a way into the world of reading and literature.

Building a community of readers takes time, experience, and a great deal of patience. Children need access to quality reading materials and time to engage with texts in the company of other readers. The experiences that we provide build the foundation for our continued exploration of literature and reading. In an article in the educational journal *Theory into Practice*, Cynthia Tyson writes, "as an educator, and member of a society that has expanded the repertoire of literacy necessary for full participation, I know that a mind 'turned off' to literature is a mind often ignored in traditional classrooms, and therefore a mind that will have fewer venues for expression" (1999, 155). The invitations I have described in this chapter are designed to "turn children on" to literature, and offer them more and more avenues for their expression.

Now that we have created an environment for readers to feel successful, found new ways to bring children and vast amounts of quality literature together, subjected our classroom libraries to important selection criteria, and made reading aloud a daily ritual, it is time to explore the elements and structures of literature in order to help children experience the language and concepts necessary for them to make deeper connections to literature.

Further Readings

CHAMBERS, AIDAN. 1996. *Tell Me: Children, Reading, and Talk*. Portland, ME: Stenhouse.

HARWAYNE, SHELLEY. 2000. *Lifetime Guarantees: Toward Ambitious Literacy Teaching*. Portsmouth, NH: Heinemann.

HINDLEY, JOANNE. 1996. *In the Company of Children*. Portland, ME: Stenhouse.

NODELMAN, PERRY. 1995. *The Pleasures of Children's Literature*. Boston: Addison-Wesley.

SHORT, KATHY. 1997. *Literature as a Way of Knowing*. Portland, ME: Stenhouse.

6
Explorations: Coming to Know Literature

We can't teach what we don't know, so anyone who doesn't know how to enjoy reading literature, thinking about it, and entering into dialogues about it shouldn't try to teach these pleasures.

PERRY NODELMAN

As we begin to explore what literature has to offer us, we need to be sure that we don't make it an unpleasant task. Exploring the elements and structures of literature, and helping children learn how to engage in "invested discussions" concerning the literature we read, should help children understand and enjoy literature more, not less. As an elementary and high school student, I can remember taking apart poetry in English class, trying to find the "hidden meanings," diagramming sentences to understand how they were constructed, and looking up vocabulary words from a novel we were assigned to read. These experiences did not add to the pleasures of reading or writing; in fact, they caused me to stop reading and writing in school altogether.

The word *exploration* means to "look into, to closely examine, to travel for the purpose of discovery." I strive to help my students make connections to stories and other texts, and help them to explore new patterns and relationships among the books and stories we have been sharing. Explorers are active readers; because of this, they develop as lifelong readers, derive pleasure from their reading selections, engage with texts throughout their lives, and determine their own purposes for reading. This type of reading as exploration can be challenging; it takes time, patience, and support. However, when readers become explorers of literature, they are empowered by their interactions with texts and take a proactive role in their development as readers.

In my classroom, when children are able to choose their own reading materials and read for extended periods of time, have begun to share their ideas and feelings with each other and respond to the texts they are reading, and have been exposed to a wide range of quality literature and are assuming the stance of active readers, it is time to help them further explore the various structures and elements that make up works of literature. I want my students to extend their stance as active readers, to begin investigating these elements of literature, to discover the layers of meaning and the literary devices authors use to craft their stories. In essence, I want them to become literary explorers.

This chapter begins with a discussion of what I have referred to as "invested discussions." With this term, I am referring to the type of interactions in our community of readers, focusing on literature, that help us come to deeper understandings from our readings, and referring to how these readings relate to our experiences and our view of the world. Some educators have referred to this as "dialogue" or "passionate attention." Whatever the terminology, this type of reading and interaction around texts places new demands on children as readers and members of a community of readers, helping them to pay close attention to others' ideas, expand their own thinking, and open up new possibilities for their interpretations.

Invested Discussions

Invested discussions are focused, informal, or open discussions where groups of students and teachers explore questions and seek out others' responses and ideas to expand the possibilities of a piece of literature. Children in these invested discussions learn to articulate their ideas about what is being read, share these ideas with each other, and appropriately address others and their diverse responses and interpretations. In our community of readers, there are many perspectives about each text we read, and we don't always agree with each other. Because of this, we must help children develop what Perry Nodelman (1996) has referred to as a child's "strength of mind" to be stimulated and developed, rather than hurt by a challenge to our ideas. By "strength of mind," Nodelman means the ability of a child to articulate and defend his or her opinions and beliefs in light of interrogation and challenge. As the classroom teacher, I need to help children learn how to discuss their different viewpoints, and disagree with one another, without feeling attacked as a person. This is one of the biggest challenges in creating invested discussions.

These invested discussions are a rich exchange of ideas, where students develop a sense of "passionate attention" about the books they are reading and the interpretations of other members of our community of readers. In these discussions, readers assume an active stance, in which meaning is constructed and revised through the social interaction of the group. It is a deeper kind of talk than simple conversation. We are invested in the discussions, caring about our ideas and the ideas of others.

Karen Smith (1990) reminds us that we want children to enter into their literary experiences and interpret them. This process of interpretation is a reciprocal process that includes growth in our human understandings, as well as our growth in literary sophistication. These discussions need to strike a balance between a focus on the text and a focus on the feelings and associations we bring to the text. We want students to be reflective, sensitive, informed explorers of literature, able to share their ideas with others, who go back to the text itself for more insight and understanding. We want readers to be "informed insiders" as they are reading literature.

As teachers, we need to be careful that we do not dominate these discussions. Offering our opinions too early in the group's discussion can result in shutting down student ideas. We need to become equal members in these discussions, offering another perspective, albeit a rather sophisticated one, to the discussion. I know I am not dominating the discussion when students feel free to question my ideas and disagree with me. This is a sign that they see me as simply another perspective on our readings.

My role is to facilitate my students' explorations of literature. Sometimes, in order to do this, I have to close my mouth and listen. Facilitating doesn't mean directing or judging every response. It means offering assistance, allowing students to come to know literature on their own terms. It means removing the impediments that block students' deeper understandings of literature, and supporting their interpretations as they explore new possibilities in their readings.

Strategies to Promote Invested Discussions

The whole-group demonstrations and explorations we do together as a community of readers are some of the most important experiences I provide to help children become invested in their discussions. During these whole-group experiences, there are several strategies or routines that I rely upon to promote our invested discussions. Many of these strategies often take considerable time to implement, but they are important because they allow more voices to be heard, more opinions to be expressed, and more attention to be focused on each others' ideas. Here are some of the strategies I have used that have been successful in my classrooms:

1. **Turn and Share:** After I have read a book to the class, I invite children to turn to a partner and share their ideas. Some children may

be reluctant to share their ideas in a large-group setting, and often find this "pair share" more inviting. After a few minutes, I ask students to share with the whole class any ideas that were discussed. Students often come back to the group and share new ideas or their partner's comments even if they have not done this before.

2. **Making Connections:** By organizing the books we read aloud to students around similar authors, themes, and genres, children begin to make connections across individual titles. This helps children compare and contrast one book or author to another and gives students more ideas to talk about. More about author and genre studies will be discussed later in this chapter.

3. **Share Circles:** When students sit in a circle and face one another, they tend to have more to say and are better positioned to listen to each other. I find that when students sit in a traditional arrangement and face me in the read aloud chair, most of the comments are directed toward the teacher, rather than toward each other. When students bounce ideas off each other, the discussion is more effective and becomes less teacher directed.

4. **Sharing Without Raising Hands:** If students can carry on a conversation without raising their hands to be recognized, they have to pay more attention to each others' comments in order to know when to speak. Because they are trying to add to the conversation, children have to be listening to each other and must learn how to politely enter a conversation. I believe that when children are used to raising their hands, they simply "tune out" until they hear their name called. This is not an easy habit to break and takes much practice, but the effects on the quality of the discussions can be remarkable.

5. **Return to the Book:** The book that was read aloud should be available to students in case they want to refer to it to make a point or check an idea. Students will sometimes ask me to turn to a certain page when making their comments. Because of the intricate nature of the illustrations and language in many of today's books, children should be allowed to revisit the text to make personal and literary connections.

6. **Attending to Children's Questions:** Traditionally, teachers ask the questions, students provide the answers, then the teacher evaluates the responses. However, children seem to ask better questions about our readings than I do. It is important to create a space where children can ask a variety of questions about the books being read. As teachers, we can learn as much, if not more, about a student's reading processes and insights into literature from the questions they ask as we can about merely the answers they give.

7. **Effective Listening:** The better listeners we are, the better we will be able to promote discussions and respond to the ideas shared by our students. If we go off in our own world because we are concerned about the math lesson we have to teach later in the day, we are not in a position to effectively promote a group discussion. We need to stay in the moment, listening for the possibilities that may arise from students' connections and comments. We always need to recognize the meanings and insights behind students' comments and be ready to help them explore new perspectives.

8. **Teacher's Willingness to Accept Possibilities:** Teachers need to know a great deal about the literature they are using in order to be successful in the reading workshop. However, this knowledge should not interfere with students' ideas and group discussions. Because we are more sophisticated in our reading abilities, and because we have had more experiences to relate to the texts we read, we need to remain open to other, often less mature, interpretations of various texts. By accepting students' approximations and their attempts to make sense of the story, we open up the discussion and allow for multiple interpretations. We should not let our interpretations narrow the possibilities that children bring to the discussion, or let our own ideas reduce our abilities to accept students' interpretations.

It is important to note that there are many factors that affect group discussions. The size of the group, the age of the students, the connections students make to the texts, background knowledge, the characteristics or structures of the text, and the cultural experiences of our students all play a role in how our discussions progress. By understanding literature and the reading process more intimately, we are in a better position to anticipate and respond to the possible interpretations and connections children bring to our discussions.

Asking Questions

One of the most influential factors in supporting or diminishing invested discussions is the type of questions we ask children during and after reading a piece of literature. Teacher's manuals and traditional education courses require teachers to be prepared to ask a series of questions after each reading to check to see if students have comprehended what they have read. I believe that in our rush to check student comprehension, we sometimes ask very inauthentic questions, and it is this type of teacher-student interaction that diminishes the opportunity for invested discussions.

If we end up playing the "20 Questions" game, asking children a barrage of "literal recall" questions to see if they have been paying attention, questions we already know the answers to, children learn that this isn't a discussion about a piece of literature; rather, it has become an inquisition, using teacher-generated questions to see if students have understood the story. Questions can certainly be a part of our community of readers, but the traditional "teacher asks, students respond" interactions can limit students' responses and change the entire focus of the discussion.

When we ask too many questions, especially ones that we already know the answers to, students come to believe that the teacher has all the answers and that it is the students' job to guess what's in the teacher's head. This type of questioning also assumes that the text is more important than the meanings students bring to, or make, during their transactions with the text. They soon realize that their ideas are not as important as their ability to answer these surface-level, literal-recall questions, and their investment in our discussions quickly fade.

When I finish reading a book, I may ask a question like "What did you think?", "What did this remind you of?", or "What did you notice?" These are honest questions, ones that I do not know the answers to. I genuinely want to know what students think, therefore I ask these questions. I will be able to tell if students have made any connections to the text by the ways in which they respond to the books being read. I don't need to ask "comprehension questions" to be able to ascertain whether students have understood the text. By asking these honest questions, children quickly learn that I care about what they think, and that I am genuinely interested in their ideas. Because of this, they begin to openly share their feelings and ideas with me and with each other. It doesn't take long for students to begin to share their ideas immediately after I finish reading, before I am able to even ask any questions.

Sometimes I ask a question in response to the ideas a student has offered. I may ask them to clarify or expand on an idea in my efforts to better understand their connections to the text. I often restate or paraphrase some of their ideas back to the group to see if I or they need to add or clarify certain points. It seems that the best questions grow out of the discussion, rather than being imposed upon it. By carefully listening to my students and working to include as many voices in the discussion as possible, I hope to create a space for these invested discussions to grow.

Charting

Another important strategy for promoting and maintaining invested discussions is charting. By writing down our ideas during these discussions, we help students make connections to other experiences with literature we have had, and begin to see the patterns and relationships between individual works of literature. I use charts for just about every part of our day. The local fire inspector and I have different beliefs about what should be allowed on classroom walls, to be sure. I think that it is important to create as many visual representations of the thinking and experiences in our classroom as we can. Charts help us to:

1. return to ideas previously discussed
2. see patterns in our experiences and discussions
3. make connections from one day to the next
4. provide continuity in our units of study
5. provide evidence of our intellectual journey
6. remember what has already been said
7. see connections between reading and writing
8. organize our ideas

When doing an author or theme study, I often begin with a large chart, sometimes referred to as a "web chart." These web charts begin with one word written along the top of the chart or in the middle, such as the name of an author or the theme of the study. Student ideas are included on "webs" that extend from this central focus. Each day as new ideas are discussed, we add to the chart any comments or ideas we feel are important. These charts help students see the connections between various ideas and help us organize our thinking. They also provide a link between reading and writing, encourage divergent thinking, and help children become invested in our discussions.

After taking these charts down from the wall at the end of the particular discussion, I fold the top of the chart around a clothes hanger. This allows me to collect these charts along a clothesline that I suspend across one corner of the room so children can take them down and use them throughout the year. It also gives me more space on the walls to—guess what?—hang more charts! I want students to be able to revisit these charts when they need to, and return to our earlier discussions throughout the year.

Another way I make a permanent record of the minilessons I teach, or the charts we have developed as a class, is to type them up and make copies for each student. My students keep these "minicharts" in a three-ring notebook along with copies of poems we have read and songs we have sung. These typed records allow students to revisit the lessons and ideas we have shared before.

In Chapter 4, I described a chart called "Impressions, Connections, and Wonderings." During our discussion of the book *Where the Wild Things Are*, I listed all of the impressions, connections, and wonderings that students shared in this discussion. This chart helps us to see where we have been in our previous discussions, and helps us to pick up where we have left off the next time we gather together.

Sometimes we go back and answer some of the wonderings, but more often than not, they are open-ended questions that remain unsolved throughout our study. I believe that it is important to allow some of these questions to remain unanswered. Not every question has an answer, or one correct answer. Actually, most good questions about literature have many possible answers. We need to help children understand that this is all right, and that we teachers don't have all the answers either.

Another chart that I use to compare more than one book is the "comparison chart." These charts list the names of different books down the left-hand column and the topics or characteristics to compare across these titles along the top row. When conducting a study about a particular theme, author, or genre, we often compare many books throughout the study. These charts help to organize the ideas in our discussions and allow students to compare the various books we have been reading.

For example, I used a comparison chart for a discussion of the various renditions of the story of the three little pigs and the wolf (see Figure 6–1). I began by asking the students to tell me the story from their memory. This version became the "traditional" version we used to begin the chart. After listing this traditional version on the chart, each day I would read a new version of the story. We read *The True Story of the Three Little Pigs* by Jon Sciezska, *The Three Little Wolves and the Big Bad Pig* by Helen Oxenberry, *The Three Little Foxes* by James Marshall, and *The Three Little Javelinas* by Susan Lowell. Each of these authors has taken a part of the story—setting or point of view, for example—and changed it to offer a new version of the story. These comparison charts also provide a good opportunity to begin discussing the elements of literature.

Elements of Literature

Like the tools a carpenter uses to build a house, authors use the elements of literature to varying degrees to construct a story. While some authors begin by creating meaningful characters, others use an extensive description of the setting to entice the reader into the story. It is the combination of these elements of literature and the interplay between them that creates a quality piece of literature. However, these elements should not be taught as an end in themselves; instead they are important aspects of the story that help the reader come to understand more intimately the craft of writing and the story created. These literary elements are the tools writers use to craft stories, and the tools readers use to gain deeper insights into the subtle intricacies of literature.

As teachers of literature, we want to call these elements of literature to the reader's conscious attention. Instinctively, most readers know that stories take place somewhere, they just may not know that this is called the "setting" and that setting has two dimensions, time and place. These elements help us to organize

Title	Characters	Setting	Ending	Changes
The Three Little Pigs (traditional)	Bad wolf Three pigs Pigs' mother	In the forest	Pigs eat the wolf, make soup	none
The True Story of the 3 Little Pigs	Innocent wolf? Three pigs	In the country	The wolf goes to jail, believes he is still innocent	The wolf's point of view; wolf tells his story
The Three Little Javelinas	Three javelinas and the coyote	Desert	The coyote goes howling off into the desert night	Everything is named after desert animals, places, plants
Yo, Hungry Wolf	The wolf and the three pigs	In the city, modern times	The wolf goes off to find something to eat in another story	Told in rap form, wolf is foolish
The Three Little Wolves and the Big Bad Pig	Three little wolves and the big bad pig	In the country	The wolves and the pig become friends and they dance together and live together	The pig is the mean guy and the wolves are afraid of him

Figure 6–1. *Three Little Pigs Comparison Chart*

how we talk about literature and give us a common vocabulary to support our class discussions. By using these elements of literature in our discussions, we enable students to move beyond the surface level of the story to understand the author's craft and the various devices they use to weave together these works of literature.

As I mentioned earlier, I don't want the study of these elements to become an end in themselves. I get nervous when I see teachers giving quizzes on what *setting*, *plot*, or *theme* means. It is more important for students to be able to discuss how the setting affects the story than it is for them to fill out a worksheet that lists the setting, main character, and theme for a particular story. The purpose of introducing these elements of literature is to develop the ability to move from labeling them to understanding how to use them to explore and discuss a piece of literature.

The books *Grand Conversations*, by Ralph Peterson and Maryann Eeds, and Perry Nodelman's *The Pleasures of Children's Literature* do an excellent job of explaining these literary elements. You will find them very helpful as you introduce your students to literary elements in your classroom discussions.

As the school year progresses, I find that wall space is always at a premium in my classroom. Because of this, I transform the large charts we create during our discussions of each element of literature into a series of construction paper posters. Each 11 × 14 sheet of construction paper lists an element of literature; they are in plain view of our read aloud area so we can refer to them during our discussions. The definitions contained in these charts develop from our experiences with the stories we have read and the background that children bring to our community of readers. They are not simply taken from the dictionary, nor are they part of any quizzes I have given. As the year progresses, these terms become a significant part of the language of our community of readers, and my testing students on these terms has never been necessary. We use them, so we know them. They become a part of the common language of our community. I use them in our discussions and expect students to do the same. The elements contained on these posters are include in Figure 6–2.

Charts for the Elements of Literature

1. <u>Parts of a Book</u>
   Cover
   Pages, words, pictures
   End pages
   Spine
   Dedication
   Index
   Table of contents
   Copyright date
   Title page: author, publisher, illustrator, title

2. <u>Author's Purpose</u>
   To express feelings
   To entertain us
   To teach us things
   Because they like to write
   Give us information
   Send message to the world
   Make us think about some things
   Make us wonder
   Make us laugh

3. <u>Setting</u>
   Where the story takes place
   The scene
   When the story takes place
   Affects the story/Mood
   Tells characters how to act

4. <u>Characters</u>
   Main character—the person the author talks the most
     about
   The story revolves around this person
   Can change during a story
   Can be an animal or a person
   Someone you follow through the book
   Supporting characters are other characters in the book

Figure 6–2. *Elements of Literature*

5. <u>Illustrations</u>
    Realistic or impressionistic
    Animation—cartoons
    Use different media—paint, sketches, watercolors, oil paints,
      pastels, crayons
    Borders or full pages
    Tells us things the words may not

6. <u>Point of View</u>
    Someone's side of the story
    Seeing things their way
    Perspective
    1st person—I went to the store
    3rd person—Two boys went to the store
    Narrators

7. <u>Plot</u>
    Events in a story
    The order things happen
    Plan of the story
    The sequence of events
    Chronological order

8. <u>Symbols</u>
    Something that represents something else
    Logos are symbols
    Peace sign, Nike
    Pictures can be symbols

9. <u>Mood</u>
    Feelings you have
    Makes you feel a certain way
    Adds to the setting
    Setting adds to the mood
    Illustrations add to the mood

10. <u>Theme</u>
    The big idea, main message
    Man vs. nature, good vs. evil, friendship, death
    Universal ideas, helps us understand ourselves
    The moral or lesson in the story

Figure 6–2. *Elements of Literature (continued)*

Fostering Connections Using Focus Units

A "focus unit" is a series of literary experiences that are organized around a central focus, be it the works of a particular author or illustrator, or a series of books in a particular genre. Sometimes referred to as "units of study," these collections of books and experiences should build upon each other, extending children's perspectives and understandings, and opening up new possibilities for connections and interpretations. These focus units, however, are different from the traditional "thematic unit" that others have written about elsewhere. Generally, thematic units are teacher-created materials that students get to work on with little or no input of their own. These traditional thematic units are usually created in the summer by groups of teachers, or they are created by commercial publishing companies and sold at teaching supply stores.

The focus units I am referring to are substantially different from these teacher-directed thematic units. I may outline possible activities, or gather together specific resources before we begin a focus unit, but the unit evolves as students read and respond to the texts I have chosen. They are part of the process, determining many of the selections to read and the experiences we will share. These are "student-centered" thematic units, so to speak, where the course of the unit and the experiences we have are based on the knowledge, previous experiences, needs, and abilities of the children in the classroom.

Reading books randomly affords students few, if any, opportunities to make connections across different titles. Although children may connect to individual titles when books are read at random, it is those connections that range across various authors, titles, illustrators, genres, and themes that seem to be the most significant in understanding literature. We want to help children to see patterns and relationships, not only in one book, but also in the genre of personal narratives, or in a series of books about issues like homelessness, freedom, or colonialism.

As described in Chapter 4, a typical unit would last two to five weeks depending on the topic or genre and its importance in the curriculum. Personal narratives have been traditionally an important genre introduced in the intermediate grades, and would therefore receive more attention than, for example, a unit on postcards. Many times a unit will cross over into our writing workshop, especially a unit such as personal narratives. As we read these books, making numerous charts about our ideas, we are trying to find the literary devices that these authors use to construct stories in this genre. By reading and exploring literature in the reading workshop, we are in a position to write from an "insider's perspective" during the writer's workshop. The growth we have as readers also affects our development as writers.

When developing a focus unit around a particular genre, I usually begin with examples of texts that fall "in the middle" of the genre. By this, I mean I begin with those prototypical or "classic" examples of a particular genre, author's work, or theme. *Owl Moon*, by Jane Yolen, is a personal narrative that I consider a classic example of this genre. This book contains beautiful language and award-winning illustrations, and it is a first-person narrative. By reading some of these classic examples of a particular genre, we are able to begin to create an understanding and a definition of what we mean by "personal narrative." Our definitions emerge from our readings, rather than being looked up in a book about literature, and remain open to revision. As we deepen our understandings of the genre or concept of these focus units, our definitions change to fit our growing perspectives.

After reading and discussing those classic examples of the theme or genre in a focus unit, I usually read some books that are "on the edge" of the genre. For example, the book *My Life with the Wave*, by Octavio Paz, has some elements of a traditional personal narrative—it is a first-person narrative, it relates the story of a child's past, and it is written in chronological order—except this story is about a boy who brings home an ocean wave to live in his house. This is a wonderful book, and usually elicits great discussions, but its events could not have actually happened. By having these discussions in our focus units, we are helping children to define and understand the concept of a particular genre or the concept's boundaries.

Some possible concepts or topics for these units are traditional genres, works of an author or illustrator, particular elements of literature, living the life of a reader, craft elements, story structures, topics or concepts from math and sciences, or themes like freedom and slavery. Some of these topics are very concrete, such as the Grand Canyon, while others are more abstract, like a unit we created on the theme "Walls and Bridges." In this particular unit, we focused on the metaphors of walls and bridges and how they are used in various pieces of literature. We ended up moving into a focus unit on architecture directly afterward because of students' interest in continuing the study of this theme and their interest in how walls and bridges are built.

During the first week or two of a particular study, I spend the majority of our time reading books and other materials that pertain to the study. I want children to be exposed to a wide variety of examples of this genre, author's writing, or concept. I would read aloud some books every day, and make many others available for students to explore. We would chart our ideas to keep track of what we have been talking about, and begin to develop preliminary definitions or insights about the focus of study. Around the third week of a study, we begin to explore the elements and literary devices that are particular to this type of literature.

We investigate the structures and craft elements that writers use to create these works. From this point, we move into trying to write in this genre or work in other forms of expression to deepen our understandings of our study.

For example, in a unit on the Grand Canyon, we took a field trip there, painted watercolors of the canyon, listened to R. Carlos Nakai's flute music, and tried to play like him on our own homemade flutes. We created brochures like the ones we received at the canyon and made our own filmstrips of our adventures. These various forms of expression help deepen children's understandings and extend their creative abilities.

During a school year, I may do as many as twenty units, some lasting four to five weeks, some only lasting one week, or we may end up only doing eight to ten larger studies. I try to blend some preplanned units, based on the requirements of my grade-level curriculum, with those "responsive" units where the topic emerges from one study and leads into another. Oftentimes, something happens in our lives that leads to a new study. I feel that this blend of preplanned experiences and ones that respond to the students' needs and interests is important. As classroom teachers, we are constantly negotiating between what we are told we have to teach, what we feel our students need, and what our students want to study.

Cornerstone Books

In creating various focus units, we select a wide assortment of books to read and explore. Rather than simply reading through book after book to begin the study, I think that it is important that we spend an extensive amount of time with one book, exploring its structures, its use of the elements of literature, and the language and illustrations contained in the text. Only after we have explored one book to the fullest do we move on to other books in the study. The books that I suggest spending extensive time with I call "cornerstone" books, because they are the foundation upon which I build the focus unit. At the beginning of Chapter 4, I described how I used Sendak's *Where the Wild Things Are* as a cornerstone book to begin the study of fictional narratives. Our extended engagement of this particular text helped us to understand the elements of fictional narrative and allowed us a foundation for comparisons with the other books in the unit.

Sometimes when using these cornerstone books, I will "disrupt" the text, take it apart or change its form, to help children see the story from a new perspectives. I do this by taking some of these books apart and displaying them in storyboard fashion, as I described with *Where the Wild Things Are*. I have also retyped parts of the book to allow students to revisit the language of the story without the accompanying illustrations. Sometimes, I am able to find books with revised covers, and this has lead to discussions about the illustrators' perspectives and how their perspectives may be different from the author's or from our own ideas. If available, I also use different versions of the same story, as with the versions of "The Three Little Pigs." Disrupting the text forces readers to attend to the structures, elements, and language of the story, as well as the actual story itself.

The books I choose to serve as cornerstone books are "classic" examples of the genre being studied, the theme of the focus unit, or important pieces by a particular author or illustrator (see Figure 6–3 for a list of suggested books).

Focus Unit: Living the Writer's Life

BAYLOR, BYRD. 1978. *The Other Way to Listen.* 1978. New York: Atheneum.

————. 1986. *I'm in Charge of Celebrations.* New York: Atheneum.

CLEARY, BEVERLY. 1983. *Dear Mr. Henshaw.* New York: Morrow, William & Company.

dePAOLA, TOMIE. 1999. *The Art Lesson.* New York: Simon & Schuster Juvenile.

FITZHUGH, LOUISE. 2000. *Harriet the Spy.* New York: Bantam Doubleday Dell Publishing.

LESTER, HELEN. 1997. *Author: A True Story.* Boston: Houghton Mifflin.

LITTLE, JEAN. 1990. *Hey World, Here I Am.* New York: Harper Trophy.

MOSS, MARISSA. 1999. *Amelia's Notebook.* Middleton, WI: Pleasant Company Publications.

WRIGHT-FRIERSON, VIRGINIA. 1996. *A Desert Scrapbook.* New York: Simon & Schuster Juvenile.

Focus Unit: Personal Narrative

BAYLOR, BYRD. 1994. *The Table Where Rich People Sit.* New York: Atheneum.

BUNTING, EVE. 1990. *The Wall.* Boston: Clarion.

————. 1993. *Fly Away Home.* Boston: Clarion.

————. 1999. *Smoky Night.* San Diego: Harcourt Brace.

MACLACHLAN, PATRICIA. 1983. *Through Grandpa's Eyes.* New York: Harper Trophy.

————. 1991. *Three Names.* New York: HarperCollins Children's.

————. 1998. *What You Know First.* New York: HarperCollins Children's.

RINGGOLD, FAITH. 1996. *Tar Beach.* Albuquerque: Dragonfly.

RYLANT, CYNTHIA. 1982. *When I Was Young in the Mountains.* New York: E. P. Dutton.

Figure 6–3. *Suggested Cornerstone Books*

RYLANT, CYNTHIA. 1993. *The Relatives Came*. New York: Aladdin Paperbacks.

THOMPSON, COLIN. 1997. *Looking for Atlantis*. Albuquerque: Dragonfly.

———. 1998. *The Paradise Garden*. New York: Knopf.

WEIDT, MARYANN. 1995. *Daddy Played Music for the Cows*. New York: Lothrop, Lee and Shepard.

WELLS, ROSEMARY. 1994. *Lucy Comes to Stay*. New York: Dial Books.

YOLEN, JANE. 1987. *Owl Moon*. New York: Philomel Books.

Focus Unit: Descriptive Language

BUNTING, EVE. 1994. *Night of the Gargoyles*. Boston: Clarion.

COWAN, CATHERINE. 1997. *My Life with the Wave*. Based on the story by Octavio Paz. New York: Lothrop, Lee and Shepard.

JOYCE, WILLIAM. 1993. *A Day with Wilbur Robinson*. New York: Harper Trophy.

———. 1996. *The Leaf Men*. New York: HarperCollins Children's.

SWOPE, SAM. 1997. *The Krazees*. New York: Farrar, Straus & Giroux.

WELLS, ROSEMARY. 1994. *Night Sounds, Morning Colors*. New York: Dial Books.

YOLEN, JANE. 1987. *Owl Moon*. New York: Philomel Books.

Focus Unit: Folktales

LACAPA, MICHAEL. 1995. *Flute Player: An Apache Folktale*. Flagstaff, AZ: Rising Moon.

LOUIE, AI-LING. 1982. *Yeh-Shen*. New York: Putnam Publishing Group.

MARTIN, RAFE. 1985. *Foolish Rabbit's Big Mistake*. New York: Putnam Publishing Group.

STEPTOE, JOHN. 1987. *Mufaro's Beautiful Daughters*. New York: Lothrop, Lee and Shepard.

WILLIAMS, JAY. 1988. *Everybody Knows What a Dragon Looks Like*. Fort Worth: Aladdin.

WISNIEWSKI, DAVID. 1996. *Golem*. Boston: Clarion.

YOUNG, ED. 1989. *Lon Po Po*. New York: Philomel Books.

Focus Unit: Historical Fiction

RINGGOLD, FAITH. 1994. *Aunt Harriet's Underground Railroad*. New York: Crown.

TSUCHIYA, YUKIO. 1988. *Faithful Elephants*. Boston: Houghton Mifflin.

TURNER, ANN WARREN. 1987. *Nettie's Trip South*. New York: Simon and Schuster.

YOLEN, JANE. 1993. *All Those Secrets of the World*. New York: Little Brown and Company.

———. 1996. *Encounter*. San Diego: Harcourt Brace.

Figure 6–3. *Suggested Cornerstone Books (continued)*

Cornerstone books are those books that you could not live without in your class-room. They are those personal favorites that you read again and again every year you teach. If I don't love the book, or my students haven't thoroughly enjoyed the book, I will be reluctant to choose it for the degree of exploration we are going to have with these cornerstone books. In my opinion, only books with quality illustrations, examples of poetic language, interesting characters, a well-developed setting, and interesting story lines make for good cornerstone books.

Cornerstone books should contain language and meanings that are accessible to the readers in your classroom. Children need to be able to understand these stories as we read them. They don't need to understand every nuance of the story the first time through, but the story shouldn't go over their heads, either. We need to be careful to choose appropriate books to serve as cornerstone books, stories that are complex, yet accessible, that students are interested in and understand when they are read to them. Since we will be spending time exploring these books, they should contain multiple layers of meaning so that students can continue to find new meanings and ideas as they interact with the story again and again.

I explore cornerstone books for this extended period of time because I believe that if we jump from new book to new book each day, without time to revisit and explore one example from the genre or theme in depth, children tend to focus on the events in the new story, rather than looking at the elements and structures of each preceding text. They want to know what happens in the story and are listening to the plot, not necessarily the language or other elements of literature. By returning to a book we have previously read, I can support discussions beyond this "plot level." Sometimes, in our rush to read through as many books as we can in a unit of study, we tend to worry about covering the curriculum, rather than uncovering it.

We spend a great deal of time with a particular cornerstone book to help children understand that a book can be read more than once and still elicit new ideas and promote interesting interpretations and discussions. I want students to realize that these multiple perspectives are not only welcome in our community, they are necessary to support the kind of invested discussions I talked about earlier in this chapter.

Reflections

As you can tell from these past two chapters, the foundation we build by reading with children, supporting invested discussions, creating charts to help us understand the connections between the books, and our experiences grouping books in focus units and exploring cornerstone books for extended periods of time makes up a large portion of the reading workshop. It is this foundation that allows us to venture even deeper into literature through literature study groups and provides the experiences students need to become more successful readers.

As teachers in literature-based classrooms using the ideas and approaches I am recommending here, we must realize that for many children this may be a new stance to reading, a new way of approaching a text, as compared to the traditional approaches used in many classrooms. We must help children get past the "find the right answer" mentality, allow them to make their own meanings while reading a text, and help them learn to share their ideas and opinions in a community of readers. It takes time and patience to help children assume the stance of explorer, but once they are there, the possibilities become endless.

Further Readings

BENEDICT, SUSAN, AND LENORE CARLISLE. 1992. *Beyond Words: Picture Books for Older Readers and Writers*. Portsmouth, NH: Heinemann.

HARWAYNE, SHELLEY. 1992. *Lasting Impressions: Weaving Literature into the Writing Workshop*. Portsmouth, NH: Heinemann.

KEENE, OLIVER, AND SUSAN ZIMMERMANN. 1997. *Mosaic of Thought: Teaching Comprehension in a Reader's Workshop*. Portsmouth, NH: Heinemann.

7

Investigations: Digging Deeper into Literature

[As teachers we need to] provide the opportunities to move beyond talk, beyond mere sharing of impressions and reactions, towards that deeper level of noticing and insight we call dialogue.

RALPH PETERSON AND MARYANN EEDS

"I hated the man in the yellow suit. He was slimy, like a used car salesman."

"Yeah he was only trying to get to the water to make money for himself. He was greedy."

"I'm kind of glad Ma Tuck killed him. He deserved it."

This is an excerpt from a discussion that my students had after reading Natalie Babbitt's *Tuck Everlasting*. This "passionate attention" to the characters and events in a piece of literature is exactly the kind of invested discussion, or dialogue, that I hope evolves over the course of the year in our literature study groups. When students become connected to what they read and can relate to the characters and events in a piece of literature, it is easier to support their "investigations" into deeper and more complex levels of understanding.

Everything that I have discussed so far in this text leads up to and supports the kind of passionate discussions Ralph Peterson and MaryAnn Eeds referred to as "grand conversations" (1990). In their book by the same name, Ralph and MaryAnn wrote about the types of interactions they believed were possible between students and teachers in response to reading quality literature. When students and teachers share their ideas and listen to the ideas of others, they become "invested" in the discussions about the books they read.

I believe that the experiences we provide *outside* of lit study groups are just as important for supporting these invested discussions as the experiences students have *within* these lit study groups. Reading aloud from a wide variety of literature, providing time and opportunities for children to read extensively on their own, exploring the elements and structures of literature, and having the support of a "joyfully literate adult" (Heath 1983) build the foundation for effective literature study groups. We should never underestimate the extent to which the experiences we provide prior to introducing lit study groups affect how children interact and discuss literature later on within these small-group structures.

Literature study groups, or lit study groups, are groups of four to seven children that come together to read and discuss their feelings, impressions, questions, and reactions to a particular piece of literature. These lit study groups revolve around a single piece of literature, usually chosen by the teacher because of its literary qualities and possibilities for discussion. In these lit study groups, personal response is valued, students become active participants in the discussion, and meanings are created and extended during the social interactions of the group. The teacher's role is to facilitate these discussions, helping students make connections, understand the structures and elements of the story, and build deeper meanings through the social interactions during the lit study group. It is within the social interactions of these lit study groups that students learn to offer ideas, evaluate other interpretations, and come to know literature and themselves more intimately.

Setting the Stage for Literature Study Groups

Before literature study groups come together in my classroom, I need to provide two separate yet parallel experiences in order to support the invested discussions necessary for successful lit study groups. First, students need experience with literature, exploring its structures and elements, and second, students need to learn how to work effectively with other students in collaborative groups. During the exploration and invitations components described in earlier chapters in this book, students are exposed to a wide variety of literature, given time for extensive independent reading, classroom discussions, and extended periods of time to explore the elements and structures of literature. These experiences provide students with the language and background they need to participate more effectively in these invested discussions. The idea sharing and the social interactions of the reading workshop help students to have the type of invested discussions that are important in lit study groups.

Along with this understanding of literature itself, students need the experience of working collaboratively in small groups with other students. They need to know how to resolve problems, listen to each other, and respect each others' ideas. Because of this belief, I have students working in small groups on various projects from the first day of school. Whether it is helping to organize the books in the classroom library, deciding how to arrange the supply center, or creating posters for the classroom walls, students need to learn to work together and gain experience doing so. It is the combination of these two parallel experiences—a deeper understanding of the elements and structures of literature and the ability to work in collaborative groups—that supports our lit study discussions.

During the first few months of school, I am on the lookout for certain signals that indicate my students are ready for the commitment necessary for successful lit study groups. By closely observing the level of sophistication of the interactions in our whole-group read aloud discussions, the understandings of literature students include in their literature response notebooks, and students' ability to work together in small groups, I get a sense of when things are coming together. Some signals that students may be ready to begin lit study groups are when students are:

1. listening to each others' ideas in our sharing circles
2. asking questions of each other, not just the teacher
3. respecting other students' opinions and ideas
4. using the language of the elements of literature in our discussions
5. beginning to recognize patterns and relationships across pieces of literature
6. developing a passion for stories
7. discussing favorite authors, genres, and titles on their own
8. reading independently or in small groups for a sustained period of time
9. referring to the charts on the elements of literature during discussions
10. solving their own problems during the reading workshop, so that the teacher can work with small groups without being constantly interrupted

These are some of the things that signal to me that the group is ready to take on the responsibility for lit study groups. Being in a lit study group is a big commitment, and making them work effectively takes a concerted effort on the part of teacher and students. A common mistake that teachers, myself included, make is starting these groups before the class is ready. Students need experience discussing literature and working with each other in collaborative groups before our lit study groups will be successful. Too often, teachers put children into groups and leave them to fend for themselves before they know what to talk about or what is expected of them. The discussions we have as a whole group and the experiences we have working in small groups support the interactions and the amount of investment we create in our lit study groups.

Generally, I don't begin lit study groups until some time in October or November. It usually takes that long before I feel students have gained the experiences with text and working with each other to make these groups successful. I watch for the signs described above, and when the community has evolved to that stage, we begin.

Getting Started

When I feel that students are ready to handle the requirements of lit study groups, I begin by having them discuss particular poems in small groups before moving on to picture books and chapter books. Because poems and picture books can be read in a single setting and can be complex enough to sustain quality discussions, I feel that these pieces work well to develop the types of discussions necessary for sustaining lit study groups that focus on chapter books or adolescent novels. As students become experienced at discussing these shorter pieces of literature and poetry, they develop the necessary understandings about literature and the abilities needed to work in small groups that are precursors to being able to handle the commitment of a lit study focusing on a chapter book.

I have often used one of my own poems to start our lit study discussions. One that has worked for me is titled "Into the Arizona Night." This poem contains poetic language and focuses on a topic that students in my classes are familiar with: the desert. I want my students to know that even though I wrote the poem, they are invited to share their own interpretations in our discussions. Just because I wrote it, doesn't mean that I have privileged access to its meaning. Each new interpretation adds to the meanings being created and sheds light on other possible interpretations. Our goal is not to reduce the poem to one "main idea"; rather, it is to expand the possible meanings and interpretations through the social interactions in these small groups.

Students are able to makes sense of this poem during the initial reading, yet it provides a variety of possible meanings that can be discussed during subsequent readings. This poem has sustained many good opening discussions in my classroom over the past several years. I want the piece of literature I choose to be rich enough for students to be able to spend time searching for more connections and deeper insights as they discuss the text, yet accessible enough to them so that they are not confused after the first reading. Because of this, it is very important to find poems and picture books that fit these requirements.

I begin by reading the poem "Into the Arizona Night" (see Figure 7–1) aloud to my class several times and provide a copy on an overhead transparency so that students can see the poem while I am reading it. We talk about how this poem affects us and what images and impressions are created in our minds as we read this

Into the Arizona Night

sand paper hills dabbed with green,
rise against the pastel sunset.

Orange fire skyline, slowly melts
into indigo stillness.

Overhead the stars crowd together,
to find their place on the celestial tapestry.

A lone coyote sings his song of freedom.

on the eve of the full moon,
we begin

the moon climbs reluctantly
into the star drenched sky

poised at the trailhead in the Superstition Mountains,
the trail unwinds before us

our invitation to sample nature,
to wander among the sights and sounds
of the Arizona night.

Frank Serafini

Figure 7–1. *"Into the Arizona Night"*

together. During this initial reading of the poem, we often mark on the transparency any particular passages or words that are powerful in evoking meanings or images. We also discuss any vocabulary that may interfere in our ability to make sense of the poem, often looking these words up in a dictionary to better understand their meanings in the poem.

After our initial discussion, the next day I provide a hard copy of the poem for each student to read and write on as I read the poem aloud again. We discuss and interpret the poem once again, looking for any new impressions or questions that may have arisen. After students have written their impressions on their individual poem sheets, we get together in small groups to share our ideas. This process, generating interpretations individually and then sharing them in small- or whole-group discussions, will be repeated throughout our lit study discussions. Students will eventually read chapter books and take notes in a "book log" independently, then use these notes to support their small-group discussions. Individual interpretations, coupled with sharing our ideas in collaborative groups, support the invested discussions we are moving toward.

As students begin to talk to each other about their reactions to the poem, I wander around from group to group listening to what is being said, trying to understand the connections and interpretations my students are making. After talking about this poem and other subsequent poems in our small groups, we pull back together and share our ideas as a whole group. This blend of individual reading with small-group and whole-group discussion allows for more voices to be heard and more ideas to be shared. I want children to feel comfortable working with each other in these small groups. I explain that everyone's ideas are important and that we need to listen to each others' ideas in order to understand the poem better.

As we are working in these "introductory" lit study groups, we stop frequently, or "pull back," to assess how our discussions are progressing. These "pull backs" help me to find out what is supporting or interfering with our lit study discussions. The level of involvement necessary for successful lit study discussions is greater than simply answering multiple-choice questions that the teacher or the basal manual pose. These discussions often become heated debates, where children disagree and passionately defend their own impressions and opinions. The social interactions in these discussions make them complex and unpredictable at times. As is written in many of the newer teacher manuals provided in commercial reading programs, "the answers may vary." No kidding! It is in fact this variety of interpretations that leads to the kinds of passionate attention and invested discussions I am looking for.

Because of the nature of these discussions, children often become overly "involved" in the action and need to be reminded of the expectations for these lit study groups. By stopping in the middle of our discussions and asking students what is happening to support or interfere with our collaborations, we help make our expectations for these invested discussions more explicit. I use a "t-chart" to write down some of the ideas offered in these "pull-back" discussions to involve students in the creation of the expectations for these lit groups. I have provided an example from one of these "t-charts" (see Figure 7–2). On the chart, we list things that have helped our discussions (Helpers) and things that have blocked our discussions (Blockers).

This list emerged from one of our initial discussion groups and we added to this list as the year progressed. Whenever our discussions "broke down," we would refer to this list to reestablish our expectations for the lit study groups. I want my students to understand what is expected of them and I want them to feel successful in these groups. By involving the students in the creation of these expectations, rather than just giving them a list of rules, students assume more responsibility for their behavior. Because of this, student become more invested in our lit study group discussions.

Helpers	Blockers
looking at each other when speaking	playing around in groups
asking each other questions	being rude
listening to what each person says	interrupting
using the book or poem for ideas	one person doing all the talking
talking so everyone can hear	not saying anything
making connections to other books	thinking you are done
trying new ideas	talking to other groups

Figure 7–2. *Lit Study Groups Discussions T-Chart*

I am very particular about the poems that I use in these introductory lit study groups. The language, meanings, and references in these particular poems must be accessible to students as they read them for the first time, yet complex enough that not all the layers of meaning can be constructed in a single reading. I want children to feel successful interpreting these poems, able to construct meaning after the first reading, but the poems must be complex enough to sustain further discussion. Other poems that I have used to launch literature discussions are

"Thunder Dragon," Harry Behn
"ten years old," Nikki Giovanni
"I, Too," Langston Hughes
"Questions," Richard Margolis
"Valentine for Ernest Mann," Naomi Shihab Nye
"By Myself," Eloise Greenfield
"If I Were in Charge of the World," Judith Viorst
"Teacher Talk," Ann Turner
"I Love the Look of Words," Maya Angelou

While I might wait until October or November to start chapter book lit study groups, we move from poems to picture books during the first few weeks of school. Supported by the whole-group discussions that take place after our read alouds, these introductory lit study group discussions, focusing on a single piece of literature, serve as a bridge between whole-group discussions and small-group chapter book lit studies.

As students feel more comfortable discussing several poems in these lit study groups, I introduce picture books to these small-group discussions in much the same manner. Besides being one of my favorite types of literature, picture books offer the reader a complex story line in a relatively short, accessible format. Also, picture books include illustrations that help children make sense of the text, while providing artwork that adds to children's interpretive possibilities. The picture books I choose are not simple stories intended for primary audiences; rather, they are more complex stories, containing poetic language and beautiful illustrations that entice children to become more intimately involved in the text. It is this sense of enjoyment and involvement that supports good lit study discussions.

I use a variety of quality picture books in the same manner as my use of the poem "Into the Arizona Night." I begin by reading the book to the whole group, and eventually provide multiple copies of books for students to explore on their own. After students have become more experienced in discussing the first few picture books, I will not read the book to them prior to their small-group discussions, and instead allow them to read it initially on their own. After a time, when students are learning to work collaboratively and becoming more invested in their discussions, I will begin with chapter book lit studies.

Selecting Literature for Lit Studies

As the discussions focusing on picture books and poems become more sophisticated and children begin living up to the expectations for the social interactions in small groups, I begin to think about what books I may choose for our chapter book lit studies. I am very picky about the kind of books I use for these lit study groups. These books must not only be wonderfully engaging stories, they must also be complex enough to foster invested discussions. I believe that these literature selections must connect to the lives and experiences of my students and help them to understand their place in the world, because the more students can connect to the stories they read and the ones read to them, the more they will become invested in our lit study discussions.

There are some books that I enjoy reading aloud to students, but would not choose for a lit study. *Tales of a Fourth Grade Nothing* by Judy Blume makes a great read aloud, but the lack of character development and rather simple story line has not made for good lit study discussions in the past. On the other hand, *Tuck Everlasting*, by Natalie Babbitt, or *Bridge to Terabithia*, by Katherine Paterson, have such poetic language, well-developed characters, elaborate settings, and intricate story lines that over the years they have supported the kind of discussions and involvement in the story necessary for successful lit study groups.

I have included a list of my favorite books I have used in my intermediate grade classrooms for lit studies (see Figure 7–3). I try to choose books that have different levels of complexity and sophistication, so that all my students will feel successful in these lit groups. This is certainly only a small sample of the books that have worked well for me in my lit studies, but I wanted to share some of my favorites so you would get a sense of the kinds of books that I have used.

It is important for me to state that I do not believe that independent reading levels should keep children out of lit study groups. By utilizing books on tape, parents as reading partners, peer helpers, or reading along with students myself, I am able to help all children understand these stories and participate in our lit study discussions. I want any child who desires to be involved in a lit study group

---

AVI. 1991. *Windcatcher*. New York: Simon & Schuster.

———. 1992. *Something Upstairs*. New York: Avon.

———. 1999. *Nothing but the Truth*. Topeka: Econo-Clad Books.

BABBITT, NATALIE. 1986. *Tuck Everlasting*. New York: Farrar, Straus & Giroux.

———. 1986. *The Eyes of the Amaryllis*. New York: Farrar, Straus & Giroux.

———. 1991. *The Search for Delicious*. New York: Farrar, Straus & Giroux.

BYARS, BETSY. 1993. *The Pinballs*. New York: HarperCollins Children.

CLEARY, BEVERLY. 1983. *Dear Mr. Henshaw*. New York: William Morrow & Company.

CONLY, JANE LESLIE. 1995. *Crazy Lady!* New York: Harper Trophy.

CREECH, SHARON. 1996. *Walk Two Moons*. New York: Harper Trophy.

GARDINER, JOHN REYNOLDS. 1988. *Stone Fox*. New York: Harper Trophy.

HADDIX, MARGARET PETERSON. 1997. *Running Out of Time*. New York: Aladdin.

JUSTER, NORTON. 1993. *The Phantom Tollbooth*. New York: Random House.

KONIGSBURG, E. L. 1998. *The View from Saturday*. New York: Aladdin.

L'ENGLE, MADELEINE. 1973. *A Wrinkle in Time*. New York: Yearling.

Figure 7–3. *Favorite Intermediate Books for Lit Studies*

LOWRY, LOIS. 1994. *The Giver*. New York: Laurel Leaf.

———. 1998. *Number the Stars*. New York: Laurel Leaf.

MacLACHLAN, PATRICIA. 1987. *Sarah, Plain and Tall*. New York: Harper Trophy.

———. 1993. *Journey*. New York: Yearling.

———. 1995. *Baby*. New York: Yearling.

O'DELL, SCOTT. 1987. *Island of the Blue Dolphins*. New York: Yearling.

———. 1995. *Zia*. New York: Yearling.

———. 1999. *Sing Down the Moon*. New York: Laurel Leaf.

PATERSON, KATHERINE. 1987. *Bridge to Terabithia*. New York: Harper Trophy.

———. 1987. *The Great Gilly Hopkins*. New York: Harper Trophy.

PAULSEN, GARY. 1987. *Hatchet*. New York: Aladdin.

———. 1993. *Nightjohn*. New York: Delacorte Press.

———. 1998. *Brian's Winter*. New York: Laurel Leaf.

RYLANT, CYNTHIA. 1995. *The Van Gogh Café*. San Diego: Harcourt Brace.

———. 1999. *The Islander*. New York: Laurel Leaf.

SACHAR, LOUIS. 2000. *Holes*. New York: Yearling.

SPINELLI, JERRY. 1997. *Crash*. New York: Random House.

———. 1998. *Wringer*. New York: Harper Trophy.

———. 2000. *Maniac Magee*. New York: Little, Brown.

STEIG, WILLIAM. 1984. *Dominic*. New York: Farrar, Straus & Giroux.

———. 1985. *The Real Thief*. New York: Farrar, Straus & Giroux.

———. 1986. *Abel's Island*. New York: Farrar, Straus & Giroux.

TAYLOR, MILDRED D. 1976. *Roll of Thunder, Hear My Cry*. New York: Puffin.

———. 1987. *The Gold Cadillac*. New York: Dial Books.

———. 1998. *The Friendship*. New York: Puffin.

WEIK, MARY HAYS. 1993. *The Jazz Man*. New York: Aladdin.

WOJCIECHOWSKA, MAIA. 1992. *Shadow of a Bull*. New York: Aladdin.

Figure 7–3. *Favorite Intermediate Books for Lit Studies (continued)*

discussion to have the opportunity to participate. Students who have not been able to read a book by themselves have made important contributions to our discussions time and again. It can be challenging to find support for all readers to participate, but it's the only option I can consider. As Carter writes, "[f]or a teacher to take it upon himself or herself that a student is too 'slow' a reader to be given a chance to tackle a good book is a serious disservice to another human being" (1986, 58).

Creating Lit Study Groups

When children are becoming more effective in their lit study discussions around poetry and picture books, as evidenced by the way they are talking and listening to each other, openly sharing their ideas, respecting others' opinions, and using the elements of literature to investigate the layers of meaning in these texts, I feel we are ready to launch chapter book lit studies.

Theoretically at least, the books themselves create the groups. To begin the process, I select five or six books from my list and introduce these books to the whole class. These introductions are called "book talks," where I give a brief introduction to the book, something like a short "commercial" trying to entice the reader into choosing that particular book. I describe what the story is about and often recommend a particular book to students I know enjoy certain types of books or topics. After doing these short book talks, I make the books available for students to browse through, giving everyone time to look through them and decide if they want to read one of these selections. About a week or so later, I post the sign-up sheets, pieces of construction paper that simply contain the name of the book and several spaces for students to sign their names. The children who want to read a particular book become the discussion group. The number of students who can sign up for a group ranges from four to seven depending on how many books I have available and the interests of my students.

All students DO NOT have to sign up for one of these books. They should only sign up for a book they *really* want to read. There will be many more opportunities to choose from other titles throughout the year. I choose books from a variety of topics and genres to allow more choices for my students. I usually begin with those books that have been successful for me in past lit studies. However, every year I add some new books that I have recently enjoyed or that other educators have recommended to me. I also allow students to make recommendations about which books to offer for lit studies during the year, but I want to be sure that their choices will provide good opportunities for discussion. I expect students to be involved with six to eight lit study groups a year. Some students are involved in more, but everyone should be in at least six.

I work with ONE book and lit study group at a time. Let me repeat myself: ONE group at a time. I do not try to keep six lit study groups going at once. I just don't think I can read the selections again and successfully support more than one group at the same time. I need to be able to read the chapter book along with the group, takes notes, and be ready to discuss my ideas, as well as facilitate the discussion within a particular group each day. By working with one group at a time, I can focus my attention on that particular group's book and discussion, and I believe this helps me do a better job of supporting these discussions. I cycle these groups through four phases, in what I am calling the "Lit Study Cycle."

The Lit Study Cycle

The lit study cycle consists of four phases: reading, discussion, creating a presentation, and having a learning celebration. Beginning with the entire class of students, which I call the "pool of readers," small groups of students reading the same book are created and progress through the lit study cycle together. The group begins by reading a book, then discussing the book along with me, preparing a presentation for the rest of the class, and then taking part in a celebration of our learning and work together. At any one time, different groups may be in different phases of the lit study cycle, but no two groups are ever meeting to discuss a book at the same time (see Figure 7–4).

Groups begin by signing up for a particular book and remain together for the entire lit study cycle. After the group has completed the cycle, students return to the pool of readers and eventually sign up for another lit study later in the year. I recommend choosing a group that you feel you know well and will be of interest to a group of students, because you want your first group to be successful, if possible.

I begin with one group that has signed up for a particular book, meet with them to talk about the expectations for the lit study, and have them sign a lit study contract (see Figure 7–5). This contract is a symbol of the level of commitment that I expect from my lit study groups, and serves as an agreement between my students and me. This contract remains in effect until the lit study group is completed. In all my years of doing these studies, only one child has ever not lived up to the contract and not finished the book, and this was because he really didn't like the book, not because he couldn't handle the expectations. The number-one priority for signing up for a book is that you really want to read it. When students really want to read the story, they are more apt to enjoy the book, read it when they are supposed to, and be more invested in the book discussions.

After reading through and signing the contract, students are given copies of the book and invited to read the first chapter, or about fifteen pages, of the book that first night. The next day, I meet with them and allow them one more chance

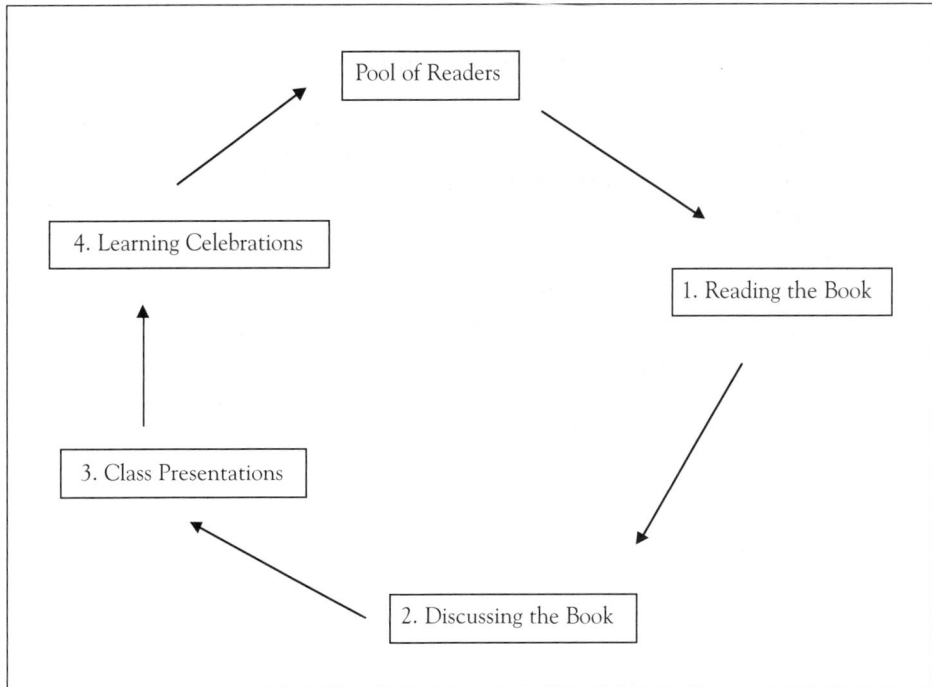

Figure 7–4. *The Lit Study Cycle*

to bow out of the group, in case they didn't like the beginning of the story. More often than not, students stick with their choice and off we go.

I give students about two weeks to read the average chapter book. These books range from 100 to 150 pages, and reading about twenty pages a night is a reasonable expectation. Some groups take longer, some shorter. Some groups I meet with while we read, and with some groups I wait until the book is finished. These decisions depend on the level of experience of the readers and the complexity of the books. When a book presents a particular challenge, for example, the technical aspects of *A Wrinkle in Time* by Madeline L'Engle, or the flashback sequences in *Walk Two Moons* by Sharon Creech, I want to be sure that students understand what is happening in the story as they are reading. I don't want them to become frustrated or confused at the beginning of a story because then the rest of the book may not make sense to them. Some stories take more time to come to understand, and some students need particular background knowledge to make sense of a story. For example, if my students were reading *Number the Stars*, by Lois Lowry, they would need some background knowledge of World War II and the Holocaust in order to make sense of this story.

Lit Study Contract

I agree to read the book _____.

I will finish the book by the time the group decides.

I will take notes in my book log and use them to help me in our discussion of the book.

I will bring my book and book log to class EVERY DAY!!!

I will PARTICIPATE in the discussion of the book.

I agree to help other students to better understand the book we have read.

I agree to work together in a group to celebrate finishing the book by creating a presentation for the class.

Date _____

Student and Teacher Names:

1.

2.

3.

4.

5.

6.

Figure 7–5. *Lit Study Contract*

1. Predictions
2. Author's Purpose or Stance
3. Ideas About the Setting
4. Personal Connections
5. Literary Connections
6. Main Character
7. Other Characters
8. Wonderings
9. Big Ideas to Share with the Group
10. Poetic/Special Language

Figure 7–6. *Book Log Headings*

To support my students as they are reading the book, I have created a "book log" for them to take notes in to bring their ideas back to the group. I have included a list of headings for sections of the book log that I have used in the past (see Figure 7–6). I want the book log to *support* students' reading and interpretations, not turn into a book report. These book logs are a place for students to take notes about their impressions, wonderings, and reactions that they want to share when we meet to discuss the book. For each heading that I have listed here, I provide about a page or half a page of space for students to write in. When we meet as a group, students are required to bring their copy of the book and their book logs to the discussion.

The Lit Study Discussions

I meet with a lit study group for about a week. Some groups have continued on longer, but most discussions continue for about five or six days. The first meeting is very casual. I ask students simply, "What did you think?" We share our initial reactions and impressions about the story, often retelling many of the parts we have enjoyed. Students may generate some questions during this initial meeting, and any of these questions that are not immediately answered are written down to be discussed later. As the first meeting ends, we decide together what topics we may want to revisit for our next meeting. Students offer many ideas, including ones about the development of a character, how the setting affects the story, particular themes that have arisen, and connections to other books and to their lives. For the next few meetings, these questions and ideas focus our discussions as we try to make sense of the piece of literature. Students are invited to go back to the text and make notes or use Post-it notes for particular places they want to refer to in the group discussion. This returning to the text supports the transactions between readers and the text. Ideas can't just be made up without support from the text, and the text can't stand alone without interpretation from the reader.

Sometimes I choose a poem or a picture book that relates to the chapter book we have been reading, which I think will extend the discussion or open up new interpretations and possibilities. For example, during a lit study on *Sadako and the Thousand Paper Cranes*, by Eleanor Coerr, I read *My Hiroshima*, a picture book by Junko Morimoto, *Hiroshima No Pika*, by Toshi Maruki, and *The Paper Crane*, by Molly Bang, to add new possibilities and interpretations to our discussions. These picture books allowed students to get more information concerning the topics in the chapter book under study, and added new perspectives to our interpretations. Using picture books and poems is just one way to extend these discussions and increase the students' involvement in the lit study discussions.

Role of the Teacher

One of the questions I am frequently asked about lit study groups is, "What is my role as the teacher in these groups?" The answer I tend to offer most often is, "Listen carefully, respond to what students are saying, and extend their ideas and connections." Now, this may not sound like much of an answer, but every group is unique, and how they interact with each other and a piece of literature is unpredictable. As teachers, we have to have faith in our students, that they will talk about their ideas, make sense of the text, and make connections to their experiences, and faith in ourselves as teachers, that we will be able to facilitate these invested discussions. We are trying to help children move beyond the "I liked the book" level of discussion and engagement. In order to do this we have to listen carefully and be able to respond in ways that takes the discussion to new levels; as Karen Smith, a professor at Arizona State University, has described to me, we must "up the ante."

As the teacher, I am a member of the group, not the sole authority and director of ideas and interpretations. As a member of the group, I share parts of the story that I didn't understand, parts that I liked and disliked, connections I have made to my own life and to other texts. I hope that by demonstrating these ways of responding to a particular text, I will help them to dig deeper into their own interpretations and make more sophisticated connections to the literature they read.

I believe that it is through sharing our ideas, not by asking a series of "critical thinking" questions, that we facilitate these discussions. I don't want my voice to be the voice of authority, but rather, one voice in the group. I do ask questions from time to time; however, they tend to be honest questions, things I really don't know the answers to, or questions that expand or clarify a student's comments. If my comments shut down the discussion, or offer a final word on what the story is "really" about, then my students' investment in these discussions becomes limited. I want to be a part of the discussion, not the center of it. As teachers, we have to be careful that our presence supports discussion, following student's insights, rather than directing them to accept our ideas. When I speak in lit study groups, I am tentative with my offerings. I try to offer speculations; for example, "I was thinking that the character might be mean spirited," or "The setting really helped me to understand the mood of the story." I often begin with, "I was thinking . . . ," or "What I thought before was . . ." This language is used to help children see that I am only one voice in the group, not *the* voice. My role is to help the conversation proceed naturally, not be controlled by the teacher. I want my expertise to sneak into these discussions, not charge through the front door.

I find that as a teacher, my role is to create an environment where students can share their ideas and listen to the ideas of others, help students make new connections to texts, and support their excavations into new layers of meaning. In this role, I am demonstrating to students how an engaged conversation works, how we enter the discussion, comment on others' ideas, and disagree politely. I want to keep the conversation going and expanding, looking for new connections and new interpretations. I often repeat students' comments back to them, asking them to expand or clarify their comments, nudging them try new perspectives. I want them to think about what they have said and where our discussion is heading. I am looking for that teachable moment, those places where I can offer assistance or help students understand a particular concept.

The best way I can describe my role in these lit study groups is as a respondent. The best preparation I can share with you is know your literature well and know your children well. This knowledge allows me a better perspective to respond to the ideas of individual students and to the direction the discussion is headed. I want to empower my students, to help them engage with the text and explore its potential meanings. I have to open up new avenues for these discussions, rather than force students down one-way streets.

Presentations and Celebrations

The most natural way we respond to our readings is by talking about what we have read. When we finish books, we tell other people about them. If someone else has read the same book, we may talk for quite awhile about our likes and dislikes. In schools, however, we often ask students to do an array of things after reading. We require them to do everything from answering a series of pre-planned questions to writing a book report. When surveyed on their preferences about reading in school, most students list these activities among their least favorite parts of reading instruction. I have to agree with them. If every time I finished a good book, I had to write a book report or make a diorama, I probably would stop reading altogether. In fact, most studies show that this is exactly what happens. Because of this, I try to limit the after-reading response "activities" to a minimum.

There are three considerations I keep in mind when inviting students to respond to texts in ways other than talking. First, is the activity authentic and relevant? Is there a model for this type of activity available in the world outside of school? Does the activity make sense to the students and have any relevance to their lives? I know that the *New York Times* contains book reviews, but not book reports. Students could write a review that other students could read, and this would seem more authentic than a book report for the teacher to check to see if the student read the book. This may not seem like much of a difference, but for me it is vital to have children respond in authentic ways.

Second, do students have a choice about how to respond to their readings? If I tell all groups that they must do a diorama, I believe it will become a chore, and not a way of extending their thinking. It is very important for students to have ownership of the activities they engage in. By asking students to offer new ways to respond to texts, and by listening to their opinions about the activities we offer, we can learn which ones are more relevant and purposeful.

Finally, these ways of responding to texts must extend students' thoughts about and understandings of the texts, not just keep them busy. Using other sign systems, such as art, drama, music, photography, or video, students can extend their understandings and ways of representing their knowledge. These responses to literature should allow students to express themselves and explore their own creativity and understandings.

After our lit study group meets for four or five discussions, students move on to the presentation phase of the lit study cycle. In this phase, students collaboratively decide on a way to present their understandings of the story to the class. Over the years, I have had students create puppet shows, skits, posters, dance performances, models, and television commercials. These activities are intended to help students come to deeper understandings about their book and their ideas related to their readings. These activities should be enjoyable and interesting for the rest of the class to watch. This is not a major part of the lit study, but it allows students to express themselves in other ways.

After the presentation, I usually buy a cake or some dessert for the group, and we get together after lunch to sit and talk. For me, sharing food and talk is an important ritual for building community and celebrating our lives and learning. After the intense discussions and the hard work put into the presentation, the children and I are ready for a celebration. Besides, I love eating good desserts.

Reflections

Literature studies have been written about in many educational books and journals in the past decade. Some of the procedures and ways of organizing student lit study discussions have become so convoluted they seem to have missed the original purpose of the discussion groups. Roles, teacher-made dialogue sheets, preplanned discussion questions, and commercially published lit study guides all try to make lit studies easier to manage. For me, the primary purpose of literature study groups is to bring readers, in this case students, together to discuss their personal impressions and reactions to a quality piece of literature. Interpretations and reactions to literature are not, nor they should be, highly predictable. These groups need to support children in developing their abilities to interpret literature share their ideas in collaborative groups, not teach children how to follow some teacher-designed discussion format. Sometimes, the less direction, the more free-dom for expression.

In order to invite students to reveal themselves to us in this manner, they need to be certain that we care about what they think, that their ideas and opinions really matter to us. When they understand this, the rest comes more easily. Once they know that we care about them and their ideas, they are more apt to share their true feelings and insights.

The support we provide for our lit study groups begins long before we choose individual books and have students sign up for groups. The foundation of these lit study groups is created during the read alouds and the ensuing discussions in our classrooms, and the exploration of the elements and structures that authors use to create these works of literature. I cannot stress enough the importance of this foundation. Students need time and patience in a supportive environment in order to excavate into deeper and more complex layers of meaning. Changing how children respond to literature, and how they interact with their peers, takes time and patience. Traditionally, schools have expected children to answer short, multiple-choice-type questions that had a right and wrong answer, or to rely on the teacher to tell them what was the correct meaning in the text. These discussion groups are very different, and in many ways more demanding. It is a challenge to invite children to reveal themselves in this manner.

Further Readings

GAMBRELL, L. B., AND J. F. ALMASSI. 1996. *Lively Discussions!: Fostering Engaged Reading.* Newark, DE: International Reading Association.

PETERSON, R., AND M. EEDS. 1994. *Grand Conversations: Literature Groups in Action.* New York: Scholastic.

SHORT, K. G., AND K. M. PIERCE. 1998. *Talking About Books.* Portsmouth, NH: Heinemann.

8

Instruction: Facilitating Children's Development as Readers

People who do not trust children to learn, or teachers to teach, will always expect a method [or program] to do the job.

FRANK SMITH

I believe that the ability to read is not something that can be directly taught to children; rather, children develop the ability to make sense of written language because of the experiences, opportunities, and support we provide for them as they engage in the act of reading. Indeed, reading "instruction" in my classroom actually takes place throughout the day. When I read aloud with children, demonstrating the way texts work, the language of stories, and the purposes for reading, it is actually part of my reading instruction, not just something we do because it is fun or because it builds community. Reading "instruction" also occurs when children self-initiate the exploration of texts and read by themselves. As central to literacy development as these demonstrations and self-initiations are, however, they are not sufficient to support children as capable, strategic readers. For more focused support, I rely on instruction that occurs in the context of actual reading events, with authentic texts. Here, I offer instruction at the point of my students' needs.

Approaches to Reading Instruction

Reading instruction takes place throughout the day during three interrelated types of instruction: 1) providing demonstrations, 2) allowing time for the self-initiated exploration of texts, and 3) direct reading instruction, where the teacher works alongside students as they interact with authentic texts and learn to use the strategies that will help them make sense of the texts they encounter. These three instructional approaches refer indirectly to the "New Zealand Model" of reading, described by Margaret Mooney (1990) as "reading to children, reading with children and reading by children" or "to, with, and by." The previous chapters have described how I use invitations and demonstrations to help students understand the power of reading and how texts work. I have also described the importance of providing time for students to explore texts on their own for extended periods of time and the importance of supporting students' investigations of literature through learning experiences such as literature study groups. In this chapter, I will look at how we support individual students' development as strategic readers.

It is important for teachers to understand that we shouldn't just abandon children in our classroom libraries to learn how to make sense of texts on their own. However, I don't believe that we have to follow the prescriptions contained in a commercial program to develop competent readers, either. The best support we can offer students is at the point of their need, in the context of actual reading events with authentic texts. I will refer to this type of direct teaching in context as "facilitated reading instruction."

Facilitated reading instruction is an approach where the teacher works alongside the reader as they engage with a text to make sense of it. The goal in this approach to reading instruction is to bring to "conscious attention" the various strategies that successful readers employ during the reading event to make sense of written language. Rather than teach "skills" in isolation, hoping they will eventually be transferred to a student's repertoire during the act of reading authentic texts, facilitated reading instruction creates experiences where teachers can support the development of particular reading strategies in the context of an actual reading event.

I believe that facilitated reading instruction is developed in two types of experiences: 1) response-centered engagements, where we teach *"into"* a child's experiences, and 2) preplanned curricular engagements, where we plan and facilitate particular classroom experiences to help develop reading strategies for our students, teaching *"in front of"* a child's experiences. Both of these types of instructional experiences should focus on the needs and abilities of individual readers as they try to make sense of authentic texts in authentic contexts.

As facilitators of children's development as readers, we are looking for those "teachable moments" where we can help children use these reading strategies in their efforts to make sense of texts. I like to refer to this as "teaching *into* children's reading." Our instruction occurs when students are engaged with texts, trying to make sense of them, and we work with them to help them develop particular reading strategies that will help them construct meaning during their engagement with a text.

Reading strategies have been referred to as "cognitive tactics," in other words, ways of thinking about and approaching a text with the goal of understanding what has been written. These strategies do not need to be learned in a predetermined sequence, nor are they taught to every child at the same time or in the same manner. Rather, the order of instruction and the resources used depend upon an individual reader's experiences with texts, their purpose for reading, the structure and elements of the text being read, and the context of the reading event. These reading strategies are intended to support children in their development as independent, lifelong readers who read for meaning from a variety of texts, for a variety of purposes, in a variety of contexts.

My approaches to facilitating the development of these strategies in young readers must align with my theoretical understandings about reading and learning, which I outlined in the second chapter. Because of these understandings, I have developed several "instructional guidelines" that help me to develop my reading strategy instruction and align these instructional practices with my theoretical understandings.

First, the goal of any reading instruction is to help the reader make sense of the story. Ultimately, I want children to be effective, independent readers, so the strategies I teach must support children's development as flexible, independent readers, capable of using a variety of strategies to make sense of texts. Second, I use authentic literature, texts that were written by authors to tell stories or provide information, not texts specifically designed for reading instruction. Books with controlled vocabulary, such as those designed to teach a common vowel pattern, are not as effective, in my opinion, for teaching reading strategies because of the lack of natural language and the focus on "phonics," not story. Third, instruction must build upon the strengths that children bring to the reading process, not their deficits. The background knowledge and life experiences that children bring to the reading event greatly influence how they perceive the reading process and how instruction should proceed. I have to closely observe my students to see what they already know before I can help them learn any new reading strategies. Fourth, reading instruction that is done in an authentic context, in response to the needs of individual readers, is more effective than an overreliance on preplanned lessons. I am constantly looking for that "teachable moment" when I can teach into a child's reading processes, helping the child at their point of need in response to their attempts during reading. Finally, my goal is to create capable, strategic, lifelong readers. Everything I do must promote the love of reading and the creation of such readers.

Along with these instructional guidelines for my reading instruction, there are four decisions I must make before I can facilitate the development of various reading strategies with my students:

1. What strategies will I teach?
2. What resources am I going to use?
3. How am I going to group students to provide reading strategy instruction?
4. What learning experiences am I going to provide to develop these strategies?

I make these decisions based on my knowledge of the reading process and the information I have gathered through the various classroom-based assessments of the students in my classroom. Because of my extensive knowledge of my individual student's needs and abilities, and of the resources I have available, I believe I am in the best position to make decisions about what strategies my students need, what experiences to provide, what resources to use, and how to group my students to develop capable, strategic readers. (I explain in a later section of this chapter how I group students. These are different groups than lit studies.) Now, the question is, "Where do we begin?"

What Strategies Do We Teach?

Before I can begin reading strategy instruction, I have to decide which strategies I am going to teach. Which ones will help children become successful, strategic readers, and which ones are they ready to understand? I believe that the best place to start is to determine what strategies children are already using. Once I understand that, I will be in a better position to decide which strategies will be the most appropriate to introduce next. To help children articulate the strategies they are already using, I use what is called a "whole-group cloze procedure." This procedure, which I will explain in detail in a moment, helps us to "uncover" those strategies we are using as we read and "give language" to the things we are doing. Since we are trying to call to "conscious attention" those things we do inside our head as we read, the cloze procedure "interrupts" the text so that we are forced to slow down and examine what strategies we are using.

I choose from among my favorite big books, books that are enlarged to allow children to see the illustrations and the written text from greater distances, which we have already read several times and enjoyed together as a class. I choose books we have read because I want this to be a low-risk, successful experience for my students. I have used the books *Is Your Mama a Llama?*, by Deborah Guarino, and *There's a Nightmare in My Closet,* by Mercer Mayer, many times for these close procedures. These two books are engaging stories, have poetic language, include well-crafted illustrations, contain repetitive language patterns, and have a highly predictable structure.

Taking one of these big books, I carefully select specific words to cover up with self-stick notes (Post-its). The words I choose force students to search the text and pictures for clues and use strategies other than "sounding it out" to predict the covered words. By covering up the whole word, I have in effect taken away the sound-symbol relationship. This forces students to rely on context, illustrations, and other clues (such as punctuation and graphic elements) to predict the words that are covered and so make sense of the text.

At the beginning of this activity, I cover words that are easily predicted from the context or illustrations; later in the activity, I try to cover words so that readers can make several predictions that would all make sense. I want them to use the available information to predict what is unavailable to them, namely the covered words. The main focus is on making sense, not on guessing the exact word that is covered.

After covering up selected words, I read the book aloud to the class, substituting the word *blank* in place of the words that are covered up. I ask students to raise their hands, rather than shouting out the answer, when they think they know what the word may be. I have them respond in this manner because I want all of my students to be able to think about their ideas before hearing other children's answers. When I call on a student, I ask them what they think the word is *and* how they figured that word out. The strategies that children are using to predict the covered word are much more important than whether they have guessed the word correctly. I want children to offer words that *make sense*, not necessarily the exact word the author chose to use. If their predictions make sense, then I know that students are using the clues provided in the text to understand the story.

The strategies that children explain they are using to predict these covered words are then listed on a chart in the classroom; they become the reading strategies that we talk about before any new ones are introduced. I have provided an example of a list that we created one year in my intermediate-grade classroom (see Figure 8–1).

Afterward, I write these strategies down on bookmarks for children to have with them as they are reading and on a wall poster for easy reference during our read aloud time. By "thinking aloud" as I am reading books to my students, I share with them how I use these strategies. These strategies need to become part of the language of our classroom so that my students will use and adopt them. They won't be used if they are discussed once and forgotten.

Because the words are completely covered up, children cannot rely on graphophonics, or the "sound-it-out" strategy. While I firmly believe that sound-symbol relationships are very important in learning to read, by the intermediate grades, children who are struggling with their reading strategies often overrely on these sound-symbol relationships, to the detriment of other equally useful strategies.

1. we read the title
2. we look at the pictures
3. we think about what would fit, make sense
4. we look at the punctuation
5. we read ahead and then go back
6. we think about the WHOLE story
7. we look at the size of the word
8. we listen for patterns or rhyming words
9. we think about what we know about the world
10. we "sound it out"

Figure 8–1. *Our Reading Strategies*

Sounding it out has been traditionally reinforced at home, taught in traditional reading programs, and, I believe, overused by inexperienced readers. I always add this strategy at the end of the list because it is a good one to use, but children need to know when and how to use it. It's not that phonics isn't a good reading strategy—the problem is that for many children, it has become their only reading strategy.

I hope that by introducing a wide variety of reading strategies, I am able to develop flexibility in children's use of reading strategies, so that children aren't relying on any one particular strategy to solve all their problems. I want students to use phonics along with other reading strategies as they try to make sense of written language. It is the effective, flexible orchestration of various reading strategies that I believe creates successful independent readers.

Although there are many lists of reading strategies available in commercial programs and educational articles, I believe that the best list to begin with is the one that you develop with your students during the whole-group cloze procedure described above. This list, however, only represents the strategies students use to make sense of a fictional narrative. The first thing I like to do after this list is created is to try the same approach with a nonfiction text, because the strategies that we use to read informational texts are different from the strategies we use for narrative texts. After doing a cloze procedure on both kinds of texts, we probably have a good list of strategies to begin with (Figure 8–1); I would add strategies to this list as they are taught during the year. Our list of strategies builds as the strategies we learn in the classroom builds.

Reading strategies do not exist separate from the context of reading. In other words, we can't teach the "skip a word and go back" strategy without being involved in reading an actual text, for an actual purpose. I don't believe that students learn these strategies using worksheets, and then go back and apply them to their reading of actual literature. These strategies emerge as readers are transacting with texts, trying to make sense of the text, depending on their purpose for reading. Because of this, I believe that teachers need to teach these strategies in the context of actual reading with authentic literature.

Rather than try to explain each individual strategy, I am going to make a list of the ones that I teach, and then move on to how I teach them and what resources I use. This list is adapted from an issue of *School Talk* (Maxim and Five 1997), published by NCTE (see Figure 8–2).

There certainly are many more things that we do as readers as we make sense of print. This list is a good start, but don't forget to ask students to share what they are doing as they read. In this way, these reading strategies are not something that comes from outside the classroom and remains unrelated to our students; rather, they emerge from our interactions with authentic reading materials.

A final strategy that has been very useful in my classroom is teaching children to ask themselves a series of questions as they read. This idea comes from the work of Marie Clay and consists of these three questions: Does it make sense? Does it sound right? Does it look right? I have added a fourth question, Why am I

1. self-correcting when something doesn't make sense
2. breaking a word into parts
3. using word analogies to predict unknown words, based on the ones already known
4. varying your reading rate
5. thinking about what would make sense
6. predicting words using the context of the story
7. using initial consonants to predict a word
8. going back to the beginning of a sentence and starting again
9. asking someone for help'
10. asking yourself questions as you read
11. stopping when things don't make sense
12. skipping a word, reading on, and then going back
13. using the dictionary to understand individual words
14. previewing a selection

Figure 8–2. *Our Reading Strategies*

reading this?, not to be a smart aleck, but to refer to the pragmatic aspects of our reading. We read texts differently depending on our purposes for reading them. I skim the newspaper on Sunday morning, but closely read a book on qualitative research while researching my dissertation. If students are asking these questions, especially "Does it make sense?", then they are probably becoming more strategic readers, trying to understand the texts they are reading.

What Resources Do We Use?

Over my years of teaching, I have developed a large collection of books and passages that I can draw from to support particular reading strategies. I keep a three-ring notebook and make overheads of excerpts from particular texts that I feel make good resources for teaching different reading strategies. I recommend that you get yourself a notebook and start collecting copies of passages and texts that you use to teach particular strategies. It doesn't take long before you have many resources available for these strategy lessons. As a reading teacher, I am constantly on the lookout for books and passages that I can use.

Predominantly, I use picture books and poems for these instructional resources, because they are complete texts that allow students to use a wide range of strategies while they are reading. For example, *Fables*, by Arnold Lobel, is one resource I use because it contains complete stories that are only a page long. These fables can be used as a cloze passage, to help children develop reading strategies like those I explained earlier, or for short retellings of a story to see if they are making sense of their reading. I prefer to use short, complete texts for retellings, rather than sections of a chapter book, so that meanings aren't left out.

Depending on the strategy I am teaching, I use books or passages that students are familiar with or ones they have not encountered. For example, if I am teaching children how to use prediction to make sense of what is coming next in a text, I would not use a text they are familiar with. On the other hand, if I am working on oral fluency, trying to help readers read in larger chunks more smoothly, I would use a text they are familiar with and one they can read easily. These decisions are made based on the strategies I am teaching, the abilities and needs of the children I am working with, and the resources I have available.

I believe that it is important to have a wide variety of texts to use for reading instruction. Texts like the Rigby, Wright Group, or *Ready to Read* series tend to focus on decoding strategies, or the graphophonic cueing system. Books like *Mrs. Wishy Washy*, by Joy Cowley, do not contain enough content to support complex discussions, but can be used to help children with one-to-one correspondence and strategies that focus on decoding or oral fluency. I believe that there is a place in reading instruction for these type of texts, but they should not be the only types of literature that children are exposed to. Children also need more complex, sophisticated texts like *Where the Wild Things Are*, the books of Chris Van Allsburg, Graeme Base, Colin Thompson, Anthony Browne, David Macauley, Natalie Babbitt, Katherine Paterson, Jane Yolen, Patricia MacLachlan, Eve Bunting, and many others to help support the construction of meaning and allow for more complex discussions about the literature they are reading.

How Do We Group for Strategy Instruction?

Theoretically, the needs of children determine how we group them together for instruction. If some students are having difficulty with a certain concept or strategy, I try to work with them as a group. In general, I introduce many strategies in whole-group settings and reinforce them in small groups or one on one. When I feel there is a particular strategy that would benefit the whole group, we may spend a good portion of the reading workshop working on that strategy. Usually, I try to keep my lessons "mini," though I do spend some days working as a whole group on some preplanned curricular engagements for the entire reading workshop. For example, the big book cloze procedure that I described earlier in this chapter took up most of one reading workshop. I have devoted other days to using reference materials, selecting books from the library, taking notes for inquiry projects, or using a particular strategy we listed on the strategy chart. I feel these lessons are important enough to take more time than the traditional five- to ten-minute "minilesson."

In the reality that plays out in the classroom, our knowledge of children is limited by our assessments, and sometimes it is difficult to know exactly what needs each student has. We make "best guesses" when we group for strategy instruction, hoping to match readers with texts that support the kinds of strategies they need. I try to work with small groups and individual students as often as possible. I feel that these settings are most conducive for reinforcing the strategies I am trying to develop in my readers. I am very careful about the lessons I decide to teach in a whole-group setting. Those lessons must be about something that everyone in the class is unfamiliar with or needs help doing, otherwise we bore some students while confusing others. I meet with strategy groups about two or three times a week and with my lit study groups on the other days. During the beginning of the year, before lit studies begin, I work with strategy groups almost every day. These groups are intermittent; they do not stay together, nor are they based on reading "levels" like traditional reading groups. These groups are based on the individual needs of students, the match between the supports and challenges of a particular text, and the amount of time and resources I have available.

How Do We Teach These Strategies?

Any reader can interact with and make sense of almost any text about things they have some experience with, if we vary the instructional approach. If the level of the text is too difficult, we read it to them. If it is easy, they can read it on their own. Most reading strategy instruction that I have been describing in this chapter falls somewhere in between these two ends. In strategy instruction, we read with them. We are trying to understand what readers are doing as they read, and support them in their efforts to make meaning as they transact with texts. We are focusing on those cognitive tactics that we use as more capable readers.

Approaches like guided reading, shared reading, student-teacher reading conferences, think alouds, and whole-group cloze procedures fall into this category of "facilitated reading instruction." There are numerous resources available that describe in detail how these approaches work, and I have listed many of them for you at the end of this chapter. I would now like to give you an example of one strategy lesson and how it would proceed in my reading workshop.

I have identified three children in my classroom who seem to be overrelying on the use of the graphophonic cueing system, the sound-symbol relationship, and are making attempts to "sound out" unknown words as their first strategy, rather than predicting what the words could be or using context to narrow down their choices before trying to sound it out. Various oral reading assessments (I will discuss these in Chapter 9) have made me believe that this particular group of students are not reading for meaning; rather, they are primarily concerned with their oral performance and often read "nonwords" aloud as they progress through their texts.

Because of the information that I have collected from my classroom-based assessments, I have decided to take a short story, an unabridged fable, and cover up several key words to use for a cloze reading procedure. Students can predict the words I have chosen to cover up by looking at the illustrations and using the context of the story. By covering up the words, I have taken away the sound-symbol relationship they have primarily used in their reading. I know that if they can't see the word, they can't try to sound it out.

I have provided photocopies of the text with these words blackened out for each of the five students in the group. We begin by looking at the title and talking about what we think a story about a mouse and a lion might be about. Students tell me that they have heard a story about a mouse that helps a lion out of a trap and this might be like that story. We begin to read the story together aloud and when we come to a word that is covered, we substitute the word blank for the covered word. I ask students to think about what they think the word might be and share with the group how they figured it out. We discuss our knowledge about the genre of fables, what we see in the illustrations, and what has happened in the story so far. I want students to concentrate on all those things that they can use besides the sound-symbol relationships. We narrow down our predictions for the covered words and I share what the actual words are. We talk about which predictions made sense and which ones didn't. I explain that I want them to ask themselves three questions when they come to a word they are unsure of, or when they get confused as they are reading: 1) Did my guess make sense?, 2) What has been going on in the story so far?, and 3) Did that sound right?

I am trying to get these readers to self-monitor what meanings they are making when they read, and to stop and reread or try something else when meaning breaks down. I am not trying to get students to ignore the sound-symbol relationships when they are reading, I just want them to have other strategies to use when that one doesn't make sense.

Reflections

No single strategy will support readers every time they get stumped. It is the flexible orchestration of a variety of strategies that leads to success in reading. We want children to develop a set of reading strategies that they can employ when trying to make sense of texts. However, the most important strategy to teach young readers is that reading is understanding. That every successful interaction with a text results in the creation of meaning. If readers do not understand this, and are unable to monitor their comprehension, they will not know when to apply an alternative reading strategy. It is because meaning "breaks down" that competent readers turn to a different reading strategy to make sense of the text. Reading is making meaning, and readers need to be able to recognize when they are no longer making sense of a text, in order to know when to apply one of these reading strategies.

Further Readings

FOUNTAS, IRENE C., AND GAY SU PINNELL. 1996. *Guided Reading: Good First Teaching for All Children*. Portsmouth, NH: Heinemann.

GOODMAN, Y., WATSON, D., AND BURKE, C. 1996. *Reading Strategies: Focus on Comprehension*. Katonah, NY: RC Owens.

MAXIM, D., AND FIVE, C. L. 1997. *School Talk: The Teaching of Reading Strategies*. Urbana, IL: National Council Teachers of English.

MOUSTAFA, MARGARET. 1997. *Beyond Traditional Phonics: Research Discoveries and Reading Instruction*. Portsmouth, NH: Heinemann.

WEAVER, CONSTANCE. 1998. *Practicing What We Know: Informed Reading Instruction*. Urbana, IL: National Council of Teachers of English.

9

Evaluations: Coming to Know
Children as Readers

*The tasks used to assess what students know and can do need to
reflect the tasks they will encounter in the world outside schools, not
merely those limited to schools themselves.*

ELLIOT EISNER

Aside from the standardized tests that I am required by law to administer to my
students a couple of times a year, there are other "classroom-based" assessments
that I utilize to come to know my students as readers and writers. However,
placing this topic in the last chapter of the book may be unintentionally mislead-
ing. Understanding children's literate abilities, needs, and interests is not
something that takes place after instruction has begun; rather, evaluation is a
reflective process that provides the teacher with the necessary information to
make curricular and instructional decisions. I assess while I am teaching, making
notes about children's understandings and abilities, and use this information
to direct my instruction. It is something that I do alongside my teaching, not after
it is over.

Unlike the large-scale, standardized tests that are used to compare schools
and school districts, or judge the effectiveness of individual literacy programs,
other teachers and I use the classroom-based assessments I will discuss in this
chapter to better understand the learners in our classrooms. Classroom-based
assessment is a process of gathering information and evaluating children's abilities
and needs in the context of the classroom environment. The primary purpose of
these assessments is to help teachers understand children's needs, interests, and
abilities for the purpose of improving teaching and learning. Classroom-based
assessments are used:

- to help children learn
- to help teachers teach
- to help teachers articulate their understandings of children's learning and growth to wider audiences (i.e., administrators, parents, legislators, departments of education, general public)

Classroom-based assessments are done in the context of learning. In other words, we don't stop teaching and learning to assess, we assess students while they are actively engaged in the experiences created in the classroom. A knowledgeable teacher, closely observing children during these authentic learning experiences, is the primary instrument for classroom-based assessment. Whether it is a formalized classroom-based assessment practice, such as running records or miscue analysis, or a teacher-designed observational checklist, these assessments are based on the close observation of children while they are learning.

The information that we gather about children comes from three interrelated sources. First, we watch children while they are learning; second, we talk to them while they are learning; and third, we gather together the products or artifacts of their learning. These are the three fundamental sources of information: observations, interactions, and artifacts. By carefully blending these three sources of information, we can construct a better understanding of the needs, interests, and abilities of our students, and then use these understandings to make decisions about the learning experiences we need to provide in our classrooms.

It is important to mention here that students are not left out of the assessment process. No longer is assessment something that we do *to* students, rather it is something that we do *with* students. Students collect artifacts in their portfolios, participate in weekly reading conferences with the teacher, prepare for student-led conferences, and reflect on their own growth and development in their journals.

Classroom-based assessments also help teachers "unpack" their criteria for evaluating students' learning and make these criteria available for students to investigate and discuss. By including students in the assessment process, we learn as much about ourselves as assessors as we do about our students. By sharing our criteria for evaluating students' work and growth, these criteria become "negotiable," changing to fit the needs of the students in our classroom and the experiences we go through.

Classroom-based assessment is an ongoing, cyclical process of gathering information, reflecting on that information, and using one's knowledge and the information gathered to make decisions about teaching and learning. In this assessment cycle, the last phase is always an action. We assess to make decisions about what to do. We use the information to provide guidance in our curriculum and instructional decisions. Assessment is not an end in itself; rather, we use it to gather information to make decisions and then gather more information to make subsequent decisions.

This chapter is not intended to be a complete course in classroom-based assessment. My intentions are instead to provide readers with an introduction to a few procedures that they can use to gather information about their students. These procedures, and the forms that I will provide in this section, are the ones that I have used in my classroom that have successfully helped me to come to know my students. The procedures that I will introduce in this chapter are

1. observational records
2. checklists
3. literature response logs
4. teacher-student conferences
5. retellings
6. miscue analysis or running records
7. reflective journals

It is my hope that with a brief introduction to these assessment procedures, and a detailed list of resources for further exploration, teachers will be able to gather the information they need to make appropriate decisions about the instructional approaches and experiences in the reading workshop.

Record Keeping

Before I begin to explain each classroom-based assessment procedure, I want to explain how I keep track of all of this information, and how I organize the paperwork to keep it manageable and easy to work with. At the beginning of the year, I take the number of students I have in the class and divide them into five groups of names. I generally go in alphabetic order because the groups are not based on ability or any other factors. I buy five large three-ring notebooks and several packets of tab dividers. In each notebook, each student gets a section and each group of students is given a name, Yellow Stars, for example. I use the names to indicate which group I will be collecting response logs from that day, or which group of students I will be having reading conferences with that day. It has been easier for me to do it this way, rather than assigning a day to each group, Monday, or Tuesday, and so on, because some days we aren't at school, and some days things get too busy to collect the required materials. By assigning groups, I merely move to the next day and collect whichever group is up next. This keeps the groups in a rotating order.

In the notebooks, each student's section begins with a student profile, which includes personal information, such as parents' names, phone numbers, names of siblings, the names of their pets, and addresses. The more I know about their backgrounds, the better I am able to help them in class. To this end, I send home a parent survey during the first week of school. This survey is included in my introductory newsletter, where I share with students and parents information about our classroom and about myself as a teacher. In the survey, I ask parents to respond to a series of questions (see Figure 9–1). I use this information to make a first contact with parents, let them know that their knowledge of their child is important, and gather information that may not be available in any other records.

After the student profiles and the student/parent survey forms are filed, I place several sheets of blank photocopier paper in each section for collecting observational records. (I will discuss these in the next section.) I also include all of the assessment forms that I will use during the course of the year. This collection of information serves as the basis for my instructional decisions; I will also use it to report to parents on report cards and in parent conferences. I believe that it is important to provide evidence for the evaluations we make and to have that evidence available to help parents and administrators understand how much we know about our students. Until these outside stakeholders begin to acknowledge our expertise as assessment instruments, we will always have to rely on the evidence provided on standardized tests.

Observational Records

Observational records, sometimes referred to as anecdotal records, are brief comments teachers write about the events and interactions they observe during the reading workshop or other part of the school day. These records are usually short, three- or four-sentence comments, describing the behaviors, learning processes, and attitudes of children in our classrooms. Each observational record should include the child's name, the date, the context of the observation, and enough information to help the teacher remember what occurred. By collecting these observational records over a period of time, teachers can use these brief records to recognize patterns in students' learning. When viewing the records of many different children together, a teacher may be able to use these observations to get insight into the needs, abilities, and challenges of the class as a whole. Many of the topics I use for my minilessons and reading strategy groups come from the information I have gathered in my observational records.

I take notes on computer mailing labels that I have separated into single sheets and placed on various clipboards throughout my room. I have about three of these clipboards, where I can take notes during different parts of the day. I just

Student Information Survey

As I mentioned in the newsletter, the more I understand about your child, the better I will be able to help develop his or her academic abilities. Please take a few moments to fill out both sides of this questionnaire so that I will be able to start to get to know your child as soon as possible. Thank you.

Name of Child:_____

1. What hobbies or special interests does your child have?

2. What does your child like to read or write at home?

3. What would you like to see developed more this year in your child?

4. What things as a parent do you feel I should know about your child?

© 2001 by Frank Serafini from *The Reading Workshop*. Portsmouth, NH: Heinemann.

Figure 9–1. *Student Information Survey*

peel them off the computer label strips and affix them to the blank sheets of paper in each child's assessment folder in chronological order. For me, it's efficient, it's easy, and most important, it's a system that I can keep up with and use consistently. I believe that whatever system you design, if it works for you, stick with it.

The system that you devise should be simple and should not require you to rewrite any records. Cutting and pasting or recopying observational records is a waste of time and takes away from a teacher's already busy schedule. The system you design should be simple to use, help you focus on every child, and allow you to make records of each subject area you want to concentrate on. It is important to develop a system that allows me to systematically focus on each child, in each area of the curriculum. Some teachers put names on the labels first so that no one is left out. When all labels are full, they start on a new set. Other teachers use a grid with student names along one side and curricular areas along the other. Whatever system you use, it should be simple and easy to manage.

I use these observational records during parent-teacher conferences to help provide vivid examples of the behaviors and learning I am sharing with parents. They also serve as a basis for my narrative report cards, or the comment section on a more traditional report card. No single record is of use until it is combined over time with a series of other observational records. In the accumulation of these observations, we begin to see patterns develop that help us make informed decisions about teaching and the experiences we should facilitate.

One last note: I once had a principal who visited my room on a regular basis. He was very supportive of my efforts and enjoyed taking one of my clipboards around with him when he was in our room. He would make notes about what he saw, lending another perspective to my observations. You may want to invite parents or other visitors to take notes about what they see, to help broaden your observations and perspectives. Everyone attends to different things during their time in the classroom and these notes help us to see things that we may have overlooked.

Checklists

Checklists are designed to help remind classroom teachers of the types of behaviors, learning processes, and understandings we are looking for during our classroom observations. They are intended to make recording our observations simpler. The information that is contained in these checklists does not contain as much contextual information and isn't as specific as the observational records, but they are easier to manage, and they provide us with an instrument that allows us to keep track of more than one student at a time in a particular curriculum area.

The actual process we go through in creating these checklists is probably more important than the finished checklist itself. As teachers spend time writing down and organizing what we feel is most important in a specific area of the curriculum, we are "unpacking" our beliefs and knowledge about that specific curricular area. This unpacking leads to better understanding of the connection between our beliefs and our instructional practices. In order for us to be able to write down what we are looking for in the reading workshop, we have to be able to articulate what it is we feel is important. This forces us to think during the reading workshop about what we feel is important, and allows us to reflect on our beliefs and open them up for revision.

For example, as I sat down to create an observational checklist for my reading workshop several years ago, I had to think about all of those things that were important for children to learn and experience during the reading workshop. I had to reflect on the school's curriculum guides, the state standards for reading instruction, current research on reading education, ideas presented in educational journals and courses at the university, and my own beliefs about reading and literature-based instruction. By reflecting on the things I valued in the reading workshop, I was able to better understand what I expected of my students and the learning experiences I would provide during this block of time (see Figure 9–2).

The items included in Figure 9–2 were written during one of my first years of teaching. Since that time, my understandings of the reading process and literate environments have grown, and the checklist has changed to reflect this. Checklists are not static documents. As the school year progresses and the teacher's knowledge base and experience with the reading process evolves, the checklist should also evolve to keep up with this change in understanding. Over my years of teaching, I have made many versions of the reading workshop checklist in Figure 9–2. The changes in my checklists directly relate to my changes in understanding about children and literacy processes.

Some students and teachers use checklists in the form of a rubric to evaluate a particular learning process or project. I have provided an example from a checklist that I designed for our literature response logs (see Figure 9–3).

I began by writing down all of those things that I felt were important for students to be including in their literature response logs. I used this checklist, along with my observational records, to keep track of my students' progress in these response logs. After writing down what I felt were important criteria for this assignment, I discussed the criteria with my students and allowed them to voice their opinions and concerns. By including my students in this process and negotiating the criteria we used to evaluate our work, I enabled my students to participate in the assessment of their work and understand what was expected of them for this particular assignment.

chooses different types of books
identifies parts of a book
reads nonfiction

can retell what has been read
makes educated predictions
uses story for clues
takes notes on reading
verifies ideas from text
recognizes genres
makes connections to real life
makes connections to other texts
recognizes favorite authors
summarizes stories
shares ideas with others

uses word identification strategies
monitors comprehension
makes corrections orally
shows inflection
oral reading is smooth, clear
uses picture clues
uses context clues

identifies elements of literature:
- setting
- theme
- mood
- symbols
- point of view
- moral
- symbols
- story structures
- author's purpose

analyzes/compares:
- character
- author's style
- author's purpose
- tensions
- illustrations

Figure 9–2. *Items on My Reading Workshop Checklist*

Format:

- includes title, author, date
- complete sentences, legibility
- answers partner's questions and teacher's questions

Responses:

- connections to own life, experiences
- connections to other books, authors, texts
- explains feelings, impressions
- compares/contrasts with other texts
- makes predictions
- confirms predictions
- asks questions during reading
- discusses elements of literature: setting, character, symbols, tension, plot, moral, genre, author's purpose, point of view, illustrations, irony, theme, mood, etc.

Sept.

Oct.

Nov.

Dec.

Jan.

Feb.

Mar.

Apr.

May

June

Figure 9–3. *Literature Response Log Checklist*

As you can see in the checklist, I provided space to make observational notes about the format I expected students to follow for each entry, as well as space for notes about the student's comments pertaining to their readings. I left space for writing down some ideas each month, although I collected the response logs about every week. I felt that writing down narrative comments was more informative than simply making a check mark. In this way, this checklist became a blend of a traditional checklist and narrative observational records.

I believe that the reflection involved in creating these checklists, and the opening up of one's beliefs and understanding about the reading process and reading instruction, is the most important aspect of these checklists. The final checklist isn't as important as the thinking that goes on in the creation of them. For this reason, I don't believe that using another teacher's checklist is as beneficial as creating your own. The checklist has to be a representation of what you as an individual teacher are looking for, not someone else. Your checklists are a reflection of your own thinking and values, and you cannot look through someone else's eyes. I have provided a copy of one of my checklists to give you an example of what it looks like, but I urge to you to take the time to create your own.

Literature Response Logs

Literature response logs, or lit logs, are notebooks that students use to record their responses to the stories and texts they are reading. I have primarily used these logs to help students keep track of their reading outside of school, to share their ideas with other students and the teacher, and as an accountability tool for making sure students are reading at home each evening. It takes time to help students understand that writing down ideas about their reading supports them as readers. These lit logs are intended to help students think about their reading, make connections across individual titles and genres, come to a better understanding of the elements of literature, and support their abilities to communicate their ideas in writing. The literature response log is designed to help students get beyond the "I liked the book" phase and explore the layers of meaning in a text.

In order for these lit logs to be successful in my classroom, I have to demonstrate what is expected and provide students with many examples before expecting students to do them effectively on their own. I do this by reading a picture book to the whole class and then demonstrating how to create a response log entry on a piece of chart paper. I do this several times during the first few weeks of school. Although students are expected to write in their lit logs from the second day of school, I know that they will need lots of demonstrations and support before they will be able to write about their reading the way I expect them to. As students begin to work in their lit logs each night for homework, I select some of these to use as examples in class. I make an overhead transparency of some of the entries that I feel are particularly insightful and share these with the class. Between the in-class demonstrations and the examples of lit logs my students have written, everyone begins to get a sense of what I expect them to write in these lit logs.

I have provided an example of the Literature Response Log format I use with my students (see Figure 9–4). I expect students to include the title, author, and date, and then write about their impressions, literary and personal connections,

Title:

Author/Illustrator:

Date:

Impressions:

Personal Connections:

Literary Connections:

Wonderings:

Figure 9–4. *Literature Response Log Format*

and wonderings they may have concerning their readings. The sections of the response log are directly related to the charts I use in my read aloud discussions presented earlier. The charts we created in the whole-group discussions serve as a demonstration for the individual student response logs. I want students to feel free to write what they feel is important, while at the same time providing a supportive framework for them to use.

There are three considerations that I need to keep in mind as I introduce these literature response logs to my students. First, I need to respond to my students' entries in the lit logs on a consistent basis. Second, I need to be aware of how students perceive this experience, and how they understand what is expected of them. Finally, I need to work with students to demonstrate how these lit logs work and make them a part of the routine of the reading workshop if I expect them to continue and be successful. Students need time to practice these lit logs, and they need a response to their efforts.

In order to provide responses to my students' efforts every day, my students share their lit logs with a "lit log partner" each morning. Students read their entries to their partners and listen to the ideas their partners have written about their books. In this way, students get feedback about their entries every day, and often become involved with the books that their partners are reading as well.

To add to the response from the lit log partners, I collect my students' lit logs each week. I read through their entries and write back to them about their ideas and any reactions I may have to their entries. I sometimes ask questions, or sometimes just make a comment about the books they are reading. Some teachers have students write their entries as a letter, and then they write back to them in the same format. Whatever the format, as long as students are receiving response to their efforts they will continue to find purpose in the lit logs.

The second consideration is that students need to perceive these logs as something that supports their reading processes and extends their thinking, not something that interferes with, or limits, their responses. I don't want students to think of these lit logs as glorified "book reports" in notebook form. If I make the lit logs a "pressured assignment," something they are doing for the teacher and not themselves, then these do not serve the purpose I have intended.

The last consideration is the importance of demonstrating how these work and sharing examples of them with your students. I often ask individual children if I can make an overhead copy of a page from their lit log to serve as an example. I share the entry with the class and we discuss what was successful about this example and what students need to do to improve their entries. Students are eager to share their work in my class, and the other students get ideas about what is expected of them for this assignment.

I want students to make sense of their reading, and these lit logs help me to see if they are in fact doing that. Rather than asking a set of comprehension questions after reading, I can get an idea about whether students are making sense of their readings by the entries they write in their lit logs. These logs serve as a forum for a written dialogue between teacher and student, and help students make sense of their readings.

Weekly Reading Conferences

Meeting with students on a weekly basis provides the classroom teacher with a wealth of information about students' reading processes, attitudes, and literacy development. These conferences also alert teachers to any challenges children are having and help us to plan instructional experiences that support these challenges. I try to meet individually with each child for a few minutes each week during the beginning of the reading workshop. I take notes about our meeting and include these notes in the record-keeping folders I described earlier in this chapter. Although these conferences are brief, they tell me a great deal about my students.

During these conferences, I ask students about their favorite books and authors, what they have been reading the past week, if they are having any problems, and what they are planning to read next. Students tell me about the books they are reading, the lit studies they are involved in, their reactions to certain reading materials, and other ideas. If students are immersed in an inquiry project, one of the things we may talk about is where to find more information for their projects. Other children may need some help discovering new titles or authors to enjoy. Whether a student is having difficulty finding books they enjoy, or having trouble choosing books that are not too difficult for them to read, these conferences can help teachers come to know their students as readers.

It seems to me that through these weekly conferences, students begin to think and reflect about their reading more consistently. Although I began these conferences to learn from my students, the conferences have affected how my students think about their own reading and their plans for future reading workshops. I have been conducting conferences like these for many years in the writing workshop, but have only recently held these conferences during the reading workshop. By spending ten to fifteen minutes at the beginning of each reading workshop conferencing with four to five children individually, I can get to each and every child at least once a week and use this information to plan my minilessons and reading curriculum. They have become one of my most effective assessment instruments.

Students know that I will be asking them about their reading and their plans for the upcoming week; they know that they need to be prepared to discuss their reading and learning with me. This has helped develop their "metacognitive" abilities and invited them to reflect on their own progress as readers. A large amount of research shows that students who are more metacognitive about their reading processes (that is, able to think about their thinking) are more successful readers. The students who were able to talk about their development as readers and were prepared for our weekly reading conferences tended to be my most successful and sophisticated readers.

Retellings

Rather than giving students lists of comprehension questions about their readings, we can learn a great deal about their reading abilities and processes, and the meanings students are constructing while reading, by asking them to retell what they have read. Retellings have long been a part of miscue analysis and running record procedures and are used to see if students are understanding what they have read.

Retellings can be unaided, no help or prompts given, or aided, where the teacher asks questions or gives hints to elicit responses. These retellings can be in oral or written form. They may come from a book that a student reads independently or one that the teacher has read to them. It is less demanding for students to be read to and allowed to respond orally than for them to be required to read the story themselves and write their ideas down. However, each of these different versions of retellings supports and challenges students in different ways and may be used for different purposes.

After reading or hearing a story, the student must explain to the teacher what the text was about or retell, as close to the original words in the story as possible, what happened in the story. Student's comprehension of a story is related to their ability to retell and talk about the events in their reading. Students that refer to exact details in the text, and can use some of the specific language of the story, have generally understood the story better than a student that just retells in generalities. When students have understood what they have read, they should be able to talk about it and retell the major aspects of the story. For a more comprehensive account of this procedure, see Brian Cambourne and Hazel Brown's book *Read and Retell* (1990). It is an excellent, easy-to-read resource on retellings. This book also provides excellent examples of texts you can use for the retellings.

Oral Reading Assessments

Miscue analysis and running records, developed by Ken Goodman and Marie Clay respectively, are formalized oral reading assessment procedures for recording and analyzing the miscues, or deviations from a text, that a student offers while reading aloud. These assessment procedures are intended to help both reading researchers and classroom teachers alike to understand the processes and thinking of readers, and to recognize patterns of reading behaviors during children's oral readings. Each procedure has developed its own particular system and set of notations for analyzing these miscues.

The basic intent of these procedures is to observe readers while reading, and to record their use of the various cueing systems: graphophonic, semantic, syntactic, and pragmatic. They are also designed to call attention to a child's reading strategies, such as sampling, predicting, cross-checking, and self-correcting. Although some of the procedures are designed for researchers and are far more complex than classroom teachers need, teachers should use these assessments to develop what Yetta Goodman has referred to in several of her presentations as a "miscue ear." By this, she means that teachers need to listen to children reading in new ways. They can no longer simply count the number of "errors" a student makes without examining the nature of the miscues and the patterns that emerge while children read. As our understandings of readers and the reading process grows, our ability to listen to readers in new ways also develops. Fluent readers naturally deviate from a text when they read. These deviations are not necessarily good or bad, correct or incorrect, until you check to see if the meaning of the passage is significantly altered by these miscues or deviations. Successful readers make sense of print, and their deviations from texts are different from those of less successful readers.

There is not enough room, nor is it the intent of this text, to elaborate on these oral reading assessments. I would like to say, however, that after I began using running records and miscue analysis in my classroom, I came to know my children as readers, and the reading process, in greater depth and understanding than ever before. I no longer listen to students read aloud the same way because of my experiences with these assessments. For an accessible introduction to miscue analysis, see Sandra Wilde's *Miscue Analysis Made Easy: Building on Student Strengths* (2000).

Reflective Notebooks

The final assessment "instrument" that I would like to share is one I have called "reflective notebooks." I have been keeping a reflective notebook for many years, in which I write down my thoughts and reflections, notes on educational articles and texts, and observations about my classroom practices. Although the reflective notebook that I use may not include specific information about a particular child, I write extensively about my classroom, my professional readings, any workshops or conferences I have attended, educational events in the local newspaper, and events at our school site.

Keeping this notebook has had a profound effect on my thinking and my teaching. I have chosen to use a blank book designed for lecture notes as my reflective notebook. I carry my notebook everywhere and fill it with my observations and reflections. Reading back through my notebooks, I have been able to see patterns of my thinking over periods of time that I wouldn't have noticed if I hadn't written them down and revisited them.

I enjoy reading through my old notebooks and making connections to the progress I have made as an educator. For me, the reflective notebook is an indispensable tool for thinking about my classroom and my teaching. In fact, the impetus and the original notes for this book came from my reflective notebook.

I am not, however, the only person in my classroom who keeps a reflective notebook. I have developed a form that my students use to reflect on their learning and share their experiences in our classroom with their parents. At the end of each day, my students and I sit down and discuss what we did and what we have learned. We begin by sharing our ideas orally as a group and then use these oral discussions to support the written reflections in our reflection logs.

The form I developed for our reflection logs is divided into different sections that correspond to the different curricular areas our day is divided into. Reading, writing, sciences, mathematics, community, and special areas are the major topics included on this form (see Figure 9–5). Students fill out one sheet each day and take home the five sheets on Friday for parents to read and respond to over the weekend.

In the forms provided in the reflection log, I have provided space for parents to respond to their children's efforts and to ask me questions or offer their comments. Every Monday, I read through each child's reflective notebook entries and respond to both the students' and the parents' entries. Sharing these reflection logs helps to include parents in our classroom learning community. Parents have shared with me how important they have found these reflection logs for helping them understand what goes on in our classroom. Over the past few years, parents have told me that when their children get home and they ask them what happened at school that day, their children sometimes reply, "Nothing much." By reading through their child's reflection logs, parents get a better understanding of what is going on in our room, and can ask their child specific questions about their day. Even though I originally designed these reflection logs to promote students' reflection about their learning, parents have found them just as important. These reflection logs have helped parents become active participants in their children's education, and have provided another means for them to communicate with me each week.

Today's Date: _____

Reading

Writing

Math

Social Studies/Science

Other Things

Community/Behavior

Figure 9–5. *Reflection Log*

Reflections

Although this chapter is near the end of this book, assessment is a reflective process that begins the first day of school and continues throughout the school year as teachers come to know their students as readers, learners, and inquirers. I use these various assessments to closely observe my students more systematically and comprehensively. I use the information gathered to guide not only individual readers' development, but also the direction of the class as a whole.

I use these assessments, along with district curriculum, state reading standards, and professional organization recommendations, to guide and create my reading curriculum and the procedures of the reading workshop. I gather information, reflect on this information, and choose particular activities and experiences to provide in my classroom. These assessments give insight into students' needs, interests, and abilities.

Further Readings

BRIDGES, LOIS. 1996. *Assessment: Continuous Learning*. Portland, ME: Stenhouse.

CAMBOURNE, BRIAN, AND HAZEL BROWN. 1990. *Read and Retell: A Strategy for the Whole Language/Natural Learning Classroom*. Portsmouth, NH: Heinemann.

JOHNSTON, PETER H. 1997. *Knowing Literacy: Constructive Literacy Assessment*. Portland, ME: Stenhouse.

RHODES, LYNN K., AND NANCY SHANKLIN. 1993. *Windows into Literacy: Assessing Learners K–8*. Portsmouth, NH: Heinemann.

STRICKLAND, KATHLEEN, AND JAMES STRICKLAND. 1999. *Making Assessment Elementary*. Portsmouth, NH: Heinemann.

WILDE, SANDRA. 2000. *Miscue Analysis Made Easy: Building on Student Strengths*. Portsmouth, NH: Heinemann.

10
Finding Our Path

"You give the Prince too many toys," said the King. "If this keeps
up, he'll turn out soft and silly."
"You give the Prince too many lessons," said the Queen. "If this
keeps up, he'll turn out dry and dusty."
"I only want what's best for him," said the King.
"But that's what I want, too," said the Queen.

NATALIE BABBITT, FROM *Bub, Or the Very Best Thing*

And so it goes. Are we teaching too much, or too little? Are we teaching children simply how to read, or are we trying to develop children's love of reading? These are the questions that we deal with every day as teachers in elementary classrooms around the globe. What should be taught, when should it be taught, and how should it be taught? It seems that teachers today are constantly trying to balance these perspectives. We want children to enjoy reading, but we also want them to be successful at it. We try to make learning enjoyable, but we want to challenge our students to grow and develop as capable human beings. How do we find the right path?

As classroom teachers, we are confronted with the pressures of external, mandated, standardized testing and the development of more complex, rigorous standards by state legislatures and professional organizations. The media often portray public schools as incompetent, and we are left to defend our decisions and the experiences children have in our classrooms. The general public wants answers to today's "literacy crisis," and the sooner the better.

Unfortunately, as teachers who work in the real world of classrooms, with real children, the "silver bullet" program that will solve all of our reading troubles will not be forthcoming. As we try to restructure our classrooms to align with our current beliefs and today's research about reading and literacy education, we are often faced with a sense of uncertainty, and we must be willing to forge ahead and undergo a certain amount of change. One professor tells you one thing, another research report suggests another, while at the same time the veteran teacher next door tells you that the things you are trying have been done before and they didn't work back then.

Change is scary for many teachers, and we want things to come together in our classrooms before the end of the first week of school. However, this rarely happens. Unsettling contradictions force us to rethink our perceptions and look closely at the experiences we try to provide our students. Life is full of ambiguities, so the texts we choose to read pose the same open degree of possibilities. We need to be able to tolerate some uncertainty if we are going to become reflective practitioners, capable of learning from our classroom experiences.

Michael Fullan (1993) has studied the change process and how it relates to educational settings and reform agendas. He says that change without vision is chaos, and that vision without change is martyrdom. Because of this, as classroom teachers we have to create a "preferred vision" of the classroom environment and experiences we want to provide children, and then be willing to accept a certain degree of uncertainty as we change and grow toward that preferred vision. It takes forward thinking, as well as time and patience, to realize our goals.

In the current political climate, I believe that we have to be able to articulate "why we do what we do" to an ever-widening range of audiences and stakeholders. Teachers can no longer hide in their classrooms and teach. We must become political advocates for the children in our classrooms and the kind of experiences we want children to have. We need to develop our abilities to talk publicly about our teaching, and learn to use the media to our advantage. In this arena, I believe, we educators need lots of help.

It seems to me that the question we need to be asking is no longer "What is the best way to teach children to read?" but "What kind of readers will our reading practices support and create?" Each program or perspective supports and develops a different vision of what a competent reader looks like. The reading workshop I have described is designed to create lifelong readers who have a passion for quality literature, feel a part of a community of readers, and are willing to share, discuss, disagree, and defend their opinions and beliefs about what they read.

The reading workshop also has to support the children who arrive at the doorsteps of our classrooms each fall. We need to begin by coming to know these children as readers, writers, thinkers, and human beings. The types of experiences we provide and the environment in which we provide them will set the tone for the types of readers we will create. I don't want my students to merely become competent readers who can read well enough to pay taxes and survive in today's society. I want to create readers who challenge taxes and participate fully in the democratic process in our country. Because of these ideas, I have to create a classroom environment where students are free to share their interpretations, interrogate the interpretations of others, and grow in their abilities to understand multiple perspectives.

Jerry Harste once shared with me a copy of a picture book that he said was a good metaphor for curriculum reform. In *Winnie the Witch*, by Korky Paul and Valerie Thomas, the central character, Winnie, lives in an all-black house with her black cat, Wilbur. After repeated problems with Wilbur blending into the background and causing Winnie to trip and fall, or to sit on him, Winnie decides to change him into a multicolored cat. His head is pink, body is purple, legs are red, and eyes are green. He climbs to the top of a tree to hide in embarrassment. Winnie eventually sees the errors of her ways, changes him back, and then proceeds to change the colors of her house instead.

In much the same way, we need to reconsider the ways we "paint" children to fit the schools and curricula that we create. By restructuring the way we teach, rather than trying to get children to fit into our old teaching models, by thinking more about children's learning than we do about our teaching, by creating classrooms where children are at the center of our practice, we are in a better position to support all of the children in becoming lifelong, successful readers.

Professional References

ATWELL, N. 1987. *In The Middle*. Portsmouth, NH: Heinemann.

CAMBOURNE, B., AND H. BROWN. 1990. *Read and Retell: A Strategy for the Whole Language/Natural Learning Classroom*. Portsmouth, NH: Heinemann.

CARTER, C. 1986. "Engaging Students in Reading." In *English Teachers at Work: Ideas and Strategies from Five Countries*, eds. S. Tchudi et al., 57–60. Portsmouth, NH: Boynton/Cook Publishers.

CLAY, M. M. 1991. *Becoming Literate: The Construction of Inner Control*. Portsmouth, NH: Heinemann.

———. 1993. *An Observation Survey of Early Literacy Achievement*. Portsmouth, NH: Heinemann.

DEWEY, J. 1938. *Experience and Education*. New York: Macmillan.

EISNER, E. 1998. *The Kinds of Schools We Need: Personal Essays*. Portsmouth, NH: Heinemann.

FULLAN, M. 1993. "Why Teachers Must Become Change Agents." *Educational Leadership* 50: 12–17.

HEATH, S. B. 1983. *Ways with Words: Language, Life, and Work in Communities and Classrooms*. New York: Cambridge University Press.

HINDLEY, J. 1996. *In the Company of Children*. Portland, ME: Stenhouse.

KAROLIDES, N. 1999. "Theory and Practice: An Interview with Louise Rosenblatt." *Language Arts* 77 (2): 158–170.

KOHN, A. 1999. *The Schools Our Children Deserve*. New York: Houghton Mifflin.

MAXIM, D. & C. L. FIVE. 1997. "The Teaching of Reading Strategies." *School Talk* 3 (1): 1–6.

MOONEY, M. 1990. *Reading to, with, and by Children*. Katonah, NY: Richard C. Owens.

NODELMAN, P. 1996. *The Pleasures of Children's Literature*. White Plains, NY: Longman.

PENNAC, D. 1999. *Better Than Life*. Portland, ME: Stenhouse.

PETERSON, R. & M. EEDS. 1990. *Grand Conversations: Literature Groups in Action*. Richmond Hill, Ontario: Scholastic.

ROSENBLATT, L. 1978. *The Reader, the Text, the Poem: The Transactional Theory of the Literary Work*. Carbondale, IL: Southern Illinois University Press.

SERAFINI, F. 1996. "Carry Me Away." *The Reading Teacher* 50 (3): 214.

SHORT, K. G. & K. M. PIERCE (eds.). 1990. *Talking About Books: Creating Literate Communities*. Portsmouth, NH: Heinemann.

SIPE, L. 1998. "How Picture Books Work: A Semiotically Framed Theory of Text-Picture Relationships." *Children's Literature in Education* 29 (2): 97–108.

SMITH, F. 1988. *Joining the Literacy Club: Further Essays into Education*. Portsmouth, NH: Heinemann.

SMITH, F. 1992. "Learning to Read: The Never-Ending Debate." *Phi Delta Kappan* 73: 432–441.

SMITH, K. 1990. "Entertaining a Text: A Reciprocal Process." In *Talking About Books: Creating Literate Communities*, eds. K. Short & K. Pierce, 17–31. Portsmouth, NH: Heinemann.

TRELEASE, J. 1989. *The New Read-Aloud Handbook*. New York: Penguin.

TYSON, C. 1999. "'Shut My Mouth Wide Open': Realistic Fiction and Social Action." *Theory into Practice* 38 (3): 155–159.

WILDE, S. 2000. *Miscue Analysis Made Easy: Building on Student Strengths*. Portsmouth, NH: Heinemann.

YUKOTO, J. 1993. "Issues in Selecting Multicultural Literature." *Language Arts* 70 (3): 156–167.

Index